FROM FAILURE TO FORTUNE

50 Impactful Lessons for the Entrepreneur

GARRY S. WHEELER

This book was originally released as *"50 Ass-Kickin' Lessons for the Enterpreneur Wannabe"* in 2018. This version has been updated and given a new title.

2024 Victory Independent Publishing.
All rights reserved.

This book or any portion thereof may not be reproduced or used in any manner whatsoever without the publisher's express written permissionexcept for the use of brief quotations in a book review.

First printing, 2024, in the United States of America.
Victory Independent Publishing
2005 SE 192nd Ave Suite 200
Camas WA 98607
www.VictoryIndependentPublishing.com
ISBN: 9798329106725

Book Cover Design and Interior Formatting by 100Covers.

DEDICATION

"Thanks to Mary, Alyssa and Jillian for your undying love and support and to my Angel Investors for your trust and faith."

TABLE OF CONTENTS

Foreword vii

The Entrepreneur ix

Chapter 1: Welcome to My Train Wreck 1

Chapter 2: The Making of an Entrepreneur Wannabe 5

Chapter 3: Yellow Brick Road Entertainment Launched
           According to What Plan? 15

Chapter 4: What a Great Idea . . . Let's Fund this Puppy! 25

Chapter 5: Time to Hire the Team 41

Chapter 6: Ready to Launch . . . Throw Me a Life Jacket 49

Chapter 7: Starting Strong, Sort of 67

Chapter 8: The Details are Devils After All 91

Chapter 9: How Do You Define Traction? 105

Chapter 10: The Aftermath: Licking my Wounds
            & Getting Back on the Horse 127

50 Impactful Lessons Learned Recap 137

About the Author 145

Appendix 149

FOREWORD

What did Sully Erna, lead singer of Godsmack, Julian Geiger, the former CEO of Aeropostale, a half dozen extremely bright Angel Investors and A&R/Marketing executives at Virgin Records, Geffen/A&M Records, Rounder Records and Disney Records have in common? **They ALL thought BandDigs.com was going to be the next Web 2.0 phenom... another Myspace or YouTube!**

Obviously, I shared the same sentiment or I wouldn't have invested my own money, sacrificed half of my earning potential and worked seven days a week to bring the concept to market over two and a half years in my late forties. How could all these knowledgeable people have been wrong and missed the mark on this one? Why wasn't this venture an over the top success? Why couldn't a first of its kind, live and interactive video website for the entertainment industry become a successful business?

Allow me to save all of you wannabe entrepreneurs a LOT of money, and of course, the pain and suffering of a startup gone bad. **Follow my journey through the ups and downs, twists and turns, and capitalize on my 50 lessons learned throughout the process.**

In the end, we will all say, "Goodbye to Yellow Brick Road Entertainment LLC" (the company I founded), but not without pause and reflection. Enjoy some of the music industry stories along the way... And most of all, prepare yourselves more effectively for managing any type of new business that you may be contemplating or are currently running. I seriously wished that I had read a book like this before I jumped into the entrepreneurial abyss. ***Please allow me to help you to avoid the same mistakes and to help you save a lot of money.***

THE ENTREPRENEUR

This book is for you if:

1. You are working in a company now and are contemplating leaving it to start your own business . . . you are looking for greener pastures . . . you found your true passion . . . you are sick of working for someone else.
2. You left a company recently and are thinking about starting your own company versus looking for another "real" job.
3. You are a student and contemplating becoming an entrepreneur after you graduate.
4. You are an entrepreneur currently struggling in your role and are looking for ideas and lessons learned that will help you succeed.
5. You failed in an entrepreneur capacity, and are seeking out someone who may have failed worse than you did to make yourself feel better. There is no shame in that!
6. You are the spouse or significant other of a recently failed entrepreneur and are trying to figure out what the hell he/she did wrong!

Okay, so let's assume you fit one of these profiles. Here are my objectives to help you address your concerns:

1. To talk those of you who are on the fence out of making a BIG mistake.

2. To help you "plungers" avoid some of the mistakes that I so effortlessly made along the way before you jump in.

3. To counsel you folks who are failing, or have already failed, by commiserating with you. Basically, I want to talk you down from the ledge.

4. Someone told me that licking my wounds in public would be really good therapy. Maybe those who can't do really *should* teach. Hmmm, novel idea.

In the following chapters, I will explain my thought process leading up to my decision to start **Yellow Brick Road Entertainment LLC** and throughout the life of it. I will then share my specific 2005-07 circa business concept, which was **BandDigs.com**, an interactive video platform/community for the music industry—a cross between Myspace and YouTube.

Subsequently, I will drill down on everything from the business plan, funding model, financials, technology, marketing analysis, customer base, vendors, and alliances, to the adjustments my team and I made, the investment banking process we followed . . . and, SPOILER ALERT, to the eventual closing of the business.

The meat in the sandwich, however, will be the brutally honest lessons learned that I will share with you. If you run with just a few of these tidbits, your ROI on this book purchase will far exceed 10,000 times.

The lessons in this book will address topics such as who you should choose for investors and why, how to write your business plan, how to know your customer, how to better develop your product or service, who not to hire and why, what types of vendors to avoid, and how to deal with angel investors, strategic funding sources, and VCs to avoid being turned down for an early round of funding. I will even share lessons I learned about myself as a person, which I hope will help you sort out your own feelings and better deal with your own struggles and doubts.

Finally, I will tell you about the aftermath—shutting down a business and facing failure for the first time. Will you be able to look at yourself in the mirror and not think of strangling yourself if you go down in flames? What will it be like dealing with your investors, friends, family, and your health if the business shuts down? Ouch... sounds rough, doesn't it? But here's the bright side: my losses may very well turn out to be your gains! And that is my goal for this book, and for you.

Hopefully, by sharing the consequences of my actions, you will be able to leverage my mistakes into a much better outcome for yourself. If it is too late for that, maybe you will find solace in relating to my distress and it will ease your own.

With all of that in mind, let's start by defining what an entrepreneur is. Here is an excerpt from an online definition of "entrepreneur":

> An **entrepreneur** is a person who has possession over a new enterprise or venture and assumes full accountability for the inherent risks and the outcome... Entrepreneur... is a term applied to the type of personality who is willing to take upon herself or himself a new venture or enterprise and accepts full responsibility for the outcome.
>
> ... They are successful because their passion for an outcome leads them to organize available resources in new and more valuable ways... A person who can efficiently manage these factors in pursuit of a real opportunity to add value in the long-run, may expand (future prospects of larger firms and businesses), and become successful.
>
> Entrepreneurship is often difficult and tricky, as many new ventures fail. Entrepreneur is often synonymous with founder. Most commonly, the term entrepreneur applies to someone who creates value by offering a product or service. Entrepreneurs often have strong beliefs about a market opportunity and organize their resources effectively to accomplish an outcome that changes existing interactions.

Picking apart the word entrepreneur is a crucial aspect of making your decision to "join the club." Indulge me while I ask you a few questions to lay the foundation:

- How much money can you afford to lose without it impacting your lifestyle, home ownership, and/or your family obligations, i.e., kid's college funding?
- Are you prepared to fail? Can you live with yourself if your venture crashes and burns? Will your spouse or significant other and children forgive you?
- What is your backup plan, and how long will it take you to implement it? How long can you afford to work for free?
- What event in your business would trigger you to start looking for another job? In other words, what would drive you to quit your new entrepreneurial venture and return to the workforce?
- What is your motivation for starting a new business?
- Do you have qualified people whom you trust lined up for hire?
- What funding sources will consider your business plan, and why do you think they will prioritize your plan over the hundreds that they look at every month?
- How well do you know the market that you are contemplating going into?
- Are you really capable of running your own business? In all honestly, could you run the company that you are working at now?
- Are you disciplined and organized? Do you procrastinate?
- Can you sell . . . and I mean, *really* sell? Not only will you need to sell your product or service, you will need to sell your ideas, which can be even harder to sell.
- Are you prepared to work for several bosses, i.e., your investors?

- When you picture running your own business, how much time do you think you will need to work each week? Are you prepared to work long hours seven days a week for the first six to twelve months?
- How will you define success in your venture?
- Have you shared your plan with at least three objective parties who understand the industry you are targeting?
- Can you succinctly describe your business concept and the ROI opportunity to a potential investor in three to five minutes?
- Are your people skills top-notch?
- How well do you deal with confrontation?

This list scratches the surface of the qualifiers for becoming an entrepreneur. Before reading further, please objectively answer these questions for yourself and your potential investors. Pause and reflect. Repeat.

Chapter 1

WELCOME TO MY TRAIN WRECK

It was 2008 and I'd just hit a milestone—I'd turned fifty years old. Instead of reflecting on my successes, however; I was licking the wounds of the biggest failure of my life. Instead of celebrating with my friends and family, I was left feeling shattered, depressed, and worthless. Hell, with my stress-induced health problems, I couldn't even hoist a martini to toast the future due to the medications that I was on. Sad sack, for sure.

"How can this be the case?" one might ask, "after enjoying thirty years of success in various business ventures by then, you had achieved a "well-to-do" status to be proud of, right?"

Right.

But that was old news by the time 2008 rolled around.

In 2005, I had decided to become an entrepreneur and go for the big win. I justified to my wife, and to myself, that life was too short not to take the risk of giving my true passion a shot—*Come on, I could be gone tomorrow!*

Tomorrow indeed arrived, almost three years later. I was still there, and so were the consequences of diving into my latest entrepreneurial venture.

Looking back, it still seems like it was a reasonable idea at the time. I was about a year into a thermal technology startup in New Hampshire, which required a lot of travel to Asia. I was the vice president of supply chain and chief information officer, and the company had just acquired two factories in China and operations in Taiwan. I was working for a great guy—a former boss, whom I respected a great deal—and making an excellent salary with lots of upside.

My then-fourteen-year-old daughter and professional singer/songwriter, Jillian, had recorded three albums by then. I was so proud of her and really into the whole recording process. I had been managing Jillian's music career since she was twelve, and I served as the executive producer on her first two albums. I subsequently hired a professional manager and entertainment attorney to help me manage what looked to be a promising career for Jillian. I had always been a huge music fan and was beyond thrilled and awed that Jillian was excelling in it.

Jillian was getting ready to go out on tour to fifty summer camps in the Northeast with her band. My wife, Mary, and I were creating a schedule of who was going to accompany Jillian to each location over the course of the summer while the other stayed home with our older daughter. This was not a trivial exercise, as the tour would end up accounting for over 10,000 miles on our SUV that summer.

With this in mind, I approached my boss about taking some time off over the summer to travel with Jillian on about thirty-five of the camp dates. By then I knew enough about the music business to realize I had discovered my true passion. The thought of coupling touring with my daughter for the summer along with my passion for music was just too intoxicating.

My boss reluctantly supported my request, although looking back I can't fathom why he did. When I think about making such a crazy request to the CEO of a frantic startup today, I just shake my head. I'm surprised the man didn't ask me if I was having some sort of breakdown or midlife crisis. Truth was, by then, I was probably on my third or fourth midlife crisis!

Nevertheless, he said yes, so I reduced my work schedule and my income in half for the summer and prepared for the tour. During the weeks leading up to the tour, I hired musicians, led the rehearsals with Jillian and the band, planned our travel, bought new equipment, invested in merchandise, and worked with Jillian's record label to plan marketing and promotion. It was an exciting time for all of us, but particularly for me. I felt twenty years younger and completely invigorated.

I was surrounded by young musicians and great music, and I got to witness my daughter blossom into a determined little performer that summer. The whole experience solidified my love of the music business and taught me a ton about running and promoting a tour like that one.

It turned out to be the turning point for me professionally and, frankly, financially for several years. It was also the impetus for my launching an entertainment-based business, **Yellow Brick Road Entertainment LLC**, in the late fall of 2005.

Chapter 2

THE MAKING OF AN ENTREPRENEUR WANNABE

I had the entrepreneur blood in me from the get-go. My father was an entrepreneur, and so was his father. Neither one particularly successful, but they had the passion, and they passed it on to me.

I worked extremely hard, mostly in the high-tech industry for 24 years and went to college evenings and weekends for over 13 years by the turn of the century. I had been operating at the executive level for the prior 15 years holding director, VP and exec VP titles. While working for large companies such as Digital Equipment Corporation and Polaroid, I had launched a couple of my own side businesses. One of them was a car leasing business and the other was a real estate development and building business. The second one was my first taste of entrepreneurial success and, I must say, it was very rewarding. Bottom line, I was extremely driven and not risk averse.

After completing night school at Harvard University with my graduate degree in 2000, everything was looking promising from a career perspective. I had a rewarding job with Aavid Thermal Technologies (the market leader in electronic cooling) and had built a great management team. I worked for a fantastic boss and had my evenings finally free from college classes. You know what they say about being on top, right?

Well, my bubble was about to burst. Aavid (then a publicly traded company) was acquired by Willis Stein Partners and taken private in the fall of 2000. My boss at the time, George Dannecker, left abruptly after having a falling-out with the new owners, and I ended up working for the new CEO. All the rules changed virtually overnight and not for the better. It was an incredibly agonizing six-plus months, and it led me to make my first "life is too short decision."

While on a family cruise to the Caribbean, drinkin' out of tall glasses with umbrellas sticking out of them, I decided that I would leave Aavid and start my own IT consulting business. I wrote my draft business concept while taking in the different islands on the cruise route. I figured it was about time that I tried becoming a full-time entrepreneur. Of course, despising my new boss at Aavid helped to spur me on.

Since I had a change-of-control clause in my Aavid contract, I left with six months' pay in my pocket. I founded Align-IT, LLC in early 2001 with a plan to provide part-time CIO services, IT project management and IT security services. I spent a couple months developing the business plan, website, marketing collateral, tools, methods, and a network of subcontractors who would work for me as projects were landed.

I then focused on sales. The basic model was based on providing objective IT advice/results. To remain objective, we steered clear of selling hardware and software. We focused on delivering high-quality projects with highly skilled resources and offered services at roughly 50% lower rates than the bigger consulting firms. On average, our consultants had fifteen or more years of experience, while most of our competitors' staff had five years or less.

One of our first customers was my old boss from Aavid, George, who had the role of CEO at a spin-off of a very large defense manufacturer. I became his part-time CIO and quickly followed up by landing two other accounts for Align-IT—so, I was off to a promising start. Because we had customers right away, I didn't need to worry about bringing in outside investors. I was able to boot-strap the company, and I treated "cash as the king." We were profitable after just a few months and remained there. I did, however, set up a credit line with the bank to help us with cash flow.

Once I had secured our first customer reference, it was pretty straight forward for me to leverage one to many by working my own personal network. By the middle of 2004, Align-IT had done over a hundred projects and had serviced seventy different customers.

As fortune would have it, one of the last customers that we serviced was yet another George Dannecker led startup called Vette Corp. George had raised millions of dollars from three different VCs to launch a new electronic cooling business, and served as the CEO.

After being involved with the planning work for Vette's launch and working closely with George again on a broader level, I paused to consider joining him full time. As much as Align-IT paid my bills for the three and a half years prior, it was very difficult work and was riskier than a full-time job would be, especially one that offered me an excellent salary, benefits, and substantial stock options—enough options to allow me to retire early should the company take off as planned. More on this later…

Allow me to digress a bit to when I finished night school a few years earlier. Finally, I had my nights free, but I just couldn't sit still. I coached basketball and softball for a couple of years for my kids, but that just didn't hook me. Due to my daughter Jillian's interest in music, I decided to take audio engineering courses in early 2003 at a local recording studio to fill up my spare time. I figured that I would be in a much better position to help her if I knew more about the recording process. While doing so, I established a great relationship with the studio owner, Steve Devino.

To receive my final training certificate, I needed to run the studio and record lead vocals. In other words, I needed a guinea pig to sing; so,

I figured why not bring Jillian into the studio to give her a taste for the experience? She was twelve years old at the time.

While I was running the mixing board for Jillian, a local producer, Jo Jo Gator, happened to be in the studio. Jo Jo had cut his teeth in the business working with the New Kids on the Block in the late '80s. Jo Jo went nuts when he heard Jillian and said, "We have to make a record for this girl. I haven't had fucking goose bumps like this listening to a performer in over ten years!"

Since Steve Devino and I enjoyed working together and found that we had a lot in common, we decided to pool our resources and start our own record label, Granite Rocks Records, LLC. Our first project together would be Jillian's debut CD.

Jo Jo would serve as the producer, and then we would look to sign additional artists and expand the label. We also invested in building the first digital download store for independent artists in New England. This project took close to a year to complete and cost thousands of dollars in development to bring to fruition. We signed up over a hundred artists for the site virtually overnight, and it looked like we might have been on to something.

We were offered CD Baby's entire digital catalog to put on our site. CD Baby was the largest distributor of independent music in the country at that time. When we sat down to analyze the workload to convert all of the files to our site and to support the expected site visitor/download volume, however, we quickly came to the conclusion that we were substantially under-resourced to handle it. Consequently, as it turned out, the only thing we were "on to" was an expensive hobby.

While focusing on Granite Rocks Records, I also served as Jillian's business manager. My wife Mary and I did everything from booking shows and creating press kits, to maintaining her website and keeping her social media sites, etc., up to date. We developed marketing materials, filled CD orders, drove Jillian to shows, ran the sound at events when needed, hired dancers and band members, sold merchandise, etc.

After Jillian performed at a very large Kid's Fair in Boston for Radio Disney in the fall of 2004, we were approached by a company that was planning to host a variety of Kid's Fairs across the country. This company wanted Jillian to become their spokesperson and a recording artist for their new indie label called WhizKidz Records.

Steve Devino was great about this. We were equal partners in Granite Rocks Records, so he could have insisted on compensation for Jillian's contract if he'd wanted to, but he cared too much about her and me to put up roadblocks. Good man!

Consequently, Jillian left Granite Rocks Records for WhizKidz Records in late 2004, and Steve and I were left with the digital download store and open discussions with several other artists that we were considering signing. Between the CD Baby realization and Jillian leaving, we decided that we just weren't capitalized well enough to do anything meaningful, so we shut down the site and the label.

Frankly, this was disheartening for me. Of course, I was excited about Jillian getting a bigger deal, but I couldn't help but feel I had wasted a lot of time and money on Granite Rocks Records, only to leave my brief stay in the music business with nothing to show for it. Steve had his recording studio, so he was still very much involved in the industry, but I was now on the sidelines.

Now let's go back to business opportunity with George Dannecker at Vette Corp. I ended up deciding in favor of joining George full-time in the summer of 2004. Ron Borelli was also there as Vette's Chairman of the Board. Ron was the former CEO/Chairman at Aavid when I had worked there for George. He was also very adept at raising venture capital and running companies. He had served as my mentor for the last few years. Not only did I see this as a great business opportunity, I thought that by joining George and Ron, I would have more spare time to devote to Jillian's career if I didn't have to run my own business. In turn, I sold Align-IT's outstanding customer contracts to an alliance partner.

You may wonder: why did I only sell the Align-IT contracts and not the business? Well, this was eye opening for me at the time. Even though we had serviced a ton of customers, had many references, had built some of our own intellectual property, and had experienced very decent financial results, the business value was inextricably linked to me personally and my relationships. Without me, there was no business and no value beyond the current contracts that we owned with customers that were legally transferable.

~~~

Now we are just sixteen months (and a few pages) away from the launch of **Yellow Brick Road Entertainment**, where all of the impactful lessons in this book materialized. The job with George and Ron was the turning point and catalyst of my *real* midlife crisis.

After the first three months at Vette, I knew I had made a serious error in judgment. I was working crazy hours, dealing with two China manufacturing plants at all hours of the night and facing extensive travel to Asia if I was going to succeed in the role. I had been to China, Hong Kong, and Taiwan several times before, so that wouldn't be new to me, but I never enjoyed going there and never fit in with the culture. I also did not enjoy being twenty-plus hours away from home. So much for having more spare time and the flexibility to manage Jillian's career.

During my last trip to mainland China, I was so sick from something that I ate that I honestly thought I was going to die in my hotel room. No one spoke English, so even getting a bottle of water was difficult. While I was in my room, I thought to myself, again: *life is too short for this*. Maybe I should have tuned out that damn voice in my head!

When 9/11 had happened a few years prior, like many, I found myself questioning many things about life and the pursuit of happiness. I even started justifying some of my decisions by contemplating another 9/11 occurring at some point that would impact me. In other words, I told myself to live my life to its fullest. You may have felt a little like this yourself during that time-period. It was such a reality check for all Americans. It motivated me to assume more financial risk and incur more debt, thinking *I could be gone tomorrow*. It left me wondering why I should work in a job that I didn't enjoy (even though work is WORK and not meant to be a vacation).

This type of thinking led me to call my wife from the office during lunch one day. I told her I was pretty much ready to jump out the window. Now remember, by then I had already convinced my boss, George, to let me cut back my hours to accompany Jillian on the camp tour that summer. Well my boss then wanted me to spend a lot more time in China as Jillian's tour winded down and, honestly, I just couldn't see myself doing it. From what I could tell, I would need to be in China about half of my time for the next several months.

I went on to tell my wife that I really needed to try to make a living somehow in the music industry. Surprisingly, she didn't think I was *that* crazy, or maybe she just concealed her feelings very well.

We agreed to talk over the weekend, but at least she was receptive to the idea and validated that life was too short for me to be so miserable. She had reason to trust me, since I had launched and operated Align-IT successfully for several years before accepting my role at Vette.

So, the little voice in my head said: *You should quit Vette Corp. Go ahead, Mister Life is Too Short. Garry, you need to figure out a way to make a living doing what you love to do. You need to create a music-related business for yourself and reap the rewards of running your own business and making a lot of money at it someday.*

Would you listen to that kind of talk from a nut job going through his second or third midlife crisis? I did, and after pleading my case further that weekend to my wife, the decision was made! I gave George my six-week notice the following week and started to plan my exit.

WTF was I thinking??? Just go out and make $175,000 to $200,000 a year like you've been making, running a who-knows-what type of music-related business—and in an industry that you really don't have much experience in. Just quit your job, and go do it man! Incomprehensible, right? I can't believe the words, "I'm leaving, George," came out of my mouth.

Ahhh, but you see, I had the infamous backup plan. My wife and I had a $200,000 home-equity line that had not been drawn upon (virgin territory). I thought, what was the worst thing that could happen? I had that to fall back on while I sorted things out. I knew "plenty" of venture capital firms, so I figured I could take a few months to develop my business plan and then get it funded so that I could pay myself a decent salary. Of course, I was also thinking that, even if I dipped into the home equity, I would eventually pay myself back when I hit it BIG.

As I mentioned previously, when I had left my job at Aavid in 2001 and started my consulting business (Align-IT), I had six months of runway due to my severance. I was fortunate to make over $150,000 a year without raising any funding, so I figured I could do it again, especially if I raised funding this time around.

So, in early September of 2005, I walked out the door of Vette Corporation, and launched my new music business career out of the basement of my home in Windham, New Hampshire.

And hence we begin with the first lesson learned. Using your own money (especially your home equity) is a very bad idea unless you can afford to flush it down the toilet. **LESSON LEARNED #1: Use other people's money and not your own to fund your startup.** You are already assuming the risk of leading a new venture and putting your career on hold in the process. Why assume the additional risk of using your own cash or, even worse, credit?

Based on my former venture capital business relationships at Aavid, Align-IT and Vette Corp., I thought VC firms would be a reliable source of funding for my new business. The fact that I wanted to be in the music business and none of the VCs I knew were in that space NEVER even entered my mind. **LESSON LEARNED #2: Don't assume your current business funding contacts will be able to help you in a different industry.** Your business might be like a square peg in a round hole for the wrong VC. I will elaborate on this in Lessons #7 and #37…

One other little detail is worth mentioning at this point. I really didn't have a clue as to what my business plan was before I gave my notice. Minor detail! I trusted myself to figure it out. **LESSON LEARNED #3: Don't trust yourself to write the plan later.** Have your plan fully fleshed out and tested with a few industry experts before you jump ship for those greener pastures. Looking back, it wouldn't have killed me to develop my plan, working on it evenings and weekends for a few months. This alone could have saved me thousands of dollars and at a bare minimum forced me to look deeper into the business model.

Chapter 3

YELLOW BRICK ROAD ENTERTAINMENT LAUNCHED... ACCORDING TO WHAT PLAN?

When I left Vette, I felt a sense of relief, but it didn't take me long to also feel a sense of fear. First, I needed an idea that could lead me to a salary of $150,000 or more in the next six months just to be able to support my family's lifestyle.

By this time, I had established a close working relationship with my daughter Jillian's manager, Joe Fletcher, on a variety of projects.

Joe seemed pretty connected in the music industry. He was primarily a concert promoter, but he managed a few recording artists as well. His company, Joe Fletcher Presents, was ranked as one of the top fifty promoters in the U.S. in 2005, producing close to two hundred concerts annually. He had expressed interest in expanding his business and adding even more artists to his roster. He also wanted to set up a record label.

I approached Joe about working with him on a strategic consulting basis. I proposed that I help him build a business plan and model that we could then use to raise VC funding. Upon raising the funding, I would then step in as a cofounder and become the COO of the expanded business. In return for doing the planning work and chasing the funding for the business, I asked him to train me on promoting concerts. I also took over managing one of Joe's bands that was based in Nashville and I hired a consultant to help me sell sponsorships for all of Joe's events.

Promoting concerts to me was one of the most gratifying business experiences of my life. I remember going to an Elton John concert a few years earlier at a local arena and thinking to myself: *If I could live my life over again, I would be a concert promoter.* It's incredibly rewarding to provide thousands of people with top-notch entertainment. The work involved in putting on a concert is diverse and challenging.

The best part of the concert business was meeting the talent at each show. You feel like a king when you paraded around with your backstage credentials and monitored the last-minute details. Of course, I also learned it is extremely tough for an independent promoter to make a profit. The competition is fierce, and the rules are stacked against you. Concert promotion is a VERY risky proposition. It is just as easy to lose your shirt on a show as it is to make any money promoting it. I never really appreciated this until I got into the details of a few shows with Joe. He had some great financial modeling tools to work with, which we used religiously when we planned the shows, but in the end, each show was a total crap shoot.

Shows that I thought would surely make money didn't, and others that I thought were dogs somehow paid off. Joe was remarkably able to navigate through the process and tolerate the financial risk somehow. He had been doing it for years and had developed a tolerance for the level of risk that he assumed every week.

As Joe pointed out to me during my first show, while I was enjoying some of the catered food backstage with the band before the concert, "The caterer is guaranteed to make money at a show. Man… the venue, sound crew, lighting guys, the advertisers, the band, the band's manager, and agent are all going to make money. The promoter, however, assumes all of the risk, puts up all the capital, and is guaranteed nothing." Promoting a concert is a lot like building a house on spec. All the subcontractors get paid, but the builder, like a promoter, may end up losing his/her shirt in the process.

Joe and I thought the way to increase profits was to acquire several other independent promoters and management companies to create critical mass and buying power (a roll up strategy). We even had a model of acquiring a small live sound company and catering business so that we were guaranteed to make some money on each show that we promoted. While working on this business plan, I experienced the good, bad, and ugly of promoting shows with performers.

Let's start with the **good**: Lily Tomlin. Joe and I had promoted a show for her in Portland, Maine. Unfortunately, the show didn't sell very well; we sold a little more than half of the seats in the theater. Before the show, Lily had agreed to do a meet-and-greet with some fans in the basement of the theater. Right after the event, Lily pulled Joe and me aside and said, "I realize you guys worked hard on this show, and I can see that ticket sales weren't that strong for whatever reason. Sometimes, I don't appeal to certain markets. I asked my manager to cut my rate in half for tonight's performance so you guys can make a little money at least." Wow, how refreshing!

On the **bad** side, Joe and I had promoted a Tim McGraw show out in Amherst, Massachusetts—8,000+ tickets sold for the concert. About a half hour before the show was to go on, the road manager called me and Joe backstage and told us that Tim wouldn't be going on if we couldn't get him an oxygen tank delivered to his dressing room before the show. BTW this requirement was not included in Tim's performance rider so we knew nothing about it. Yeah, thirty minutes beforehand, we were threatened that the show wouldn't go on—and, to boot, in Massachusetts, you need a permit to use oxygen. I scrambled and called the local fire department. I explained that I used to be a volunteer fireman and knew what I was about to ask them was going to be tough to pull off. After fully explaining the predicament, they came through for us and sent a tank over to the venue. It was such a relief to get that much support in the moment. They were probably worried that there would be a riot if Tim didn't go on!

Now the **ugly**: We promoted a Willie Nelson concert at the University of New Hampshire. In order to make any money on the show, due to Willie's high rate, we had to sell sponsorships for the event. We had permission in our contract with Willie to do so, as well as an agreement with him to appear in a meet-and-greet before the show with people of our choice. One of the local banks agreed to be the lead sponsor of the show in return for private time for their top customers with Willie before the concert.

Well, fifteen minutes before the bank event was scheduled to start, Willie's road manager told me that Willie wasn't feeling well and he wasn't going to do the meet-and-greet. Of course, I replied that we had a contract with Willie, had made commitments to the sponsor, and really needed Willie to appear, even if it was just a short appearance. His manager proceeded to tell me that if I didn't let it go, then Willie wouldn't do the show at all. His exact words were, "Do you want us to pack up our fucking stuff and leave?" Talk about a slap in the face. I then had to deliver the news to our sponsor and let them know we would be refunding their money for the event. This cost us $35,000!

Again, Willie and everyone else associated with the show made money, but Joe and I suffered the loss. To add insult to injury, we discovered that Willie had held his own private Fan Club event during the same time that he was supposed to do the meet-and-greet for us. Nice guy, eh? The only saving grace for me is that I have trashed Willie to anyone who would listen to me for the last ten years. It hasn't replaced the $35K, but it has made for great storytelling!

Once Joe and I had the basic construct of our working relationship ironed out, I dove in with both feet as Joe's strategic consultant. I created an elaborate business plan based on acquiring several smaller promoters, management firms, etc. I then created presentation summaries and new service offerings, helped with concert operations, and began parading the plan around to funding sources in the greater Boston area.

After each funding proposal presentation, however, I discovered just how much I didn't know about the concert and artist management business. The margins were lousy, the risks were high, and the guarantees of us discovering new artists that would make us a tidy profit were nonexistent. To make matters worse, even though Joe had been in business for fifteen years, his financials were not very strong. He also didn't have a track record of discovering new talent that went on to make it big, so we didn't have that to leverage as evidence that we knew what we were doing.

Bottom line, none of my personal funding contacts wanted in, even after we entertained some of them at our bigger concerts and impressed them with our ability to put on great shows. The business model was flawed, and to make matters worse, my VC contacts were not the least bit interested in the industry.

After about ten unsuccessful meetings and a fair amount of tension between me and Joe on the business model and financial plan, I came to the realization that I was barking up the wrong tree. So, after Thanksgiving of 2005, I totally shifted gears. I told Joe that I needed to move on to Plan B and founded **Yellow Brick Road Entertainment (YBR)** on my own.

Fortunately, this time, *I really did have a plan B.*

While managing Jillian's music career, I had become very aware of websites such as Friendster, Myspace, Xanga, and other online social communities popular in 2005. I had also stumbled onto YouTube.com before most people had even heard of it. We had a page for Jillian on Myspace, and she had thousands of friends. It wasn't very long before she couldn't keep up with the friend requests and postings, so we had interns take care of the responses for her.

Knowing that we had interns taking care of Jillian's Myspace page, I figured that most artists with any type of following were probably doing the same. This was the germination of Plan B.

Remember, my goal when I left my cushy job; I wanted to make a living in the music industry. Unfortunately, right out of the gate, I learned that unless I was willing to start at the bottom and really learn the business, I was going to need to come up with another angle. So here it goes: I decided to leverage my IT background and create a technology play that would resonate with my VC contacts. This would then enable me to make a living in an industry that I was passionate about.

My basic idea was to create a Web 2.0 cloud-based community for fans in large numbers to interact with their favorite bands over the Internet utilizing webcams. I figured, this way, fans would know they were really communicating with the bands and not communicating with the bands' interns or managers. Additionally, the bands could cover more ground by communicating en masse to their fans versus one at a time on sites like Myspace.

Moreover, the fans could then pay to have their video chat recorded with the band and download a copy of their conversation as a keepsake to watch on their computer or their video iPod. Wow, I was pretty proud of myself when the idea came to me. So much so that I called my patent attorney to do a little research to see if I was in unchartered territory.

In addition to letting fans chat with bands, I wanted to give bands the ability to broadcast themselves live using a digital video camera from anywhere that they could access the Internet. I figured that with the expansion of high-speed Internet and the improvements in online video tools, that there would be enough bandwidth available to support live broadcasts.

My thinking here was that bands could expand their fan base globally without even leaving their rehearsal space. Fans could be taken behind the scenes at clubs, recording studios, concerts, and even on tour buses. Basically, anywhere the band wanted to take their fans, the fans could go.

Surrounding these video tools, I envisioned an online social networking community where fans and bands could build their own identity similar to their pages on Myspace, upload songs/videos, and link to their other social media sites. Now mind you, all I had was a concept and a few PowerPoint slides at this point, basically cool vaporware.

I quickly convinced myself that this was a great idea. I shifted all my attention to creating a business plan and a comprehensive summary presentation that would lay the groundwork for building a prototype and allow me to raise enough capital to support the buildout and launch of the site.

Looking back, this was probably the most excited I had been about anything in years. Not since I had served as Jillian's executive producer on her first album several years prior, had I felt so energized.

I dedicated myself to the project and worked seven days a week on the details. As soon as I had written enough documentation about how the site would function, I started networking with a few folks under nondisclosure to try to find a company that could build a prototype of the site for me. I needed something to demonstrate to potential investors and to share with some bands to get their feedback on my approach.

I followed up with my patent attorney, and he concluded that there were no apparent conflicts for me to worry about. A green light.

I needed to come up with a name for this interactive video community so that I could register the domain name and engage a graphic expert to design the logo and the site layout, color scheme, etc. I came up with a handful of different names and tested them with a few folks, but I have to give my daughter Jillian credit for the name that I ended up going with. The site **BandDigs.com** was born out of this process and would be owned and operated by **Yellow Brick Road Entertainment**.

You can see excerpts from my original business plan's executive summary in the appendix of this book (Exhibit A), to get a feel for how I defined the opportunity. See the slide below which summarized where I saw the music industry in 2006.

MUSIC INDUSTRY DYNAMICS

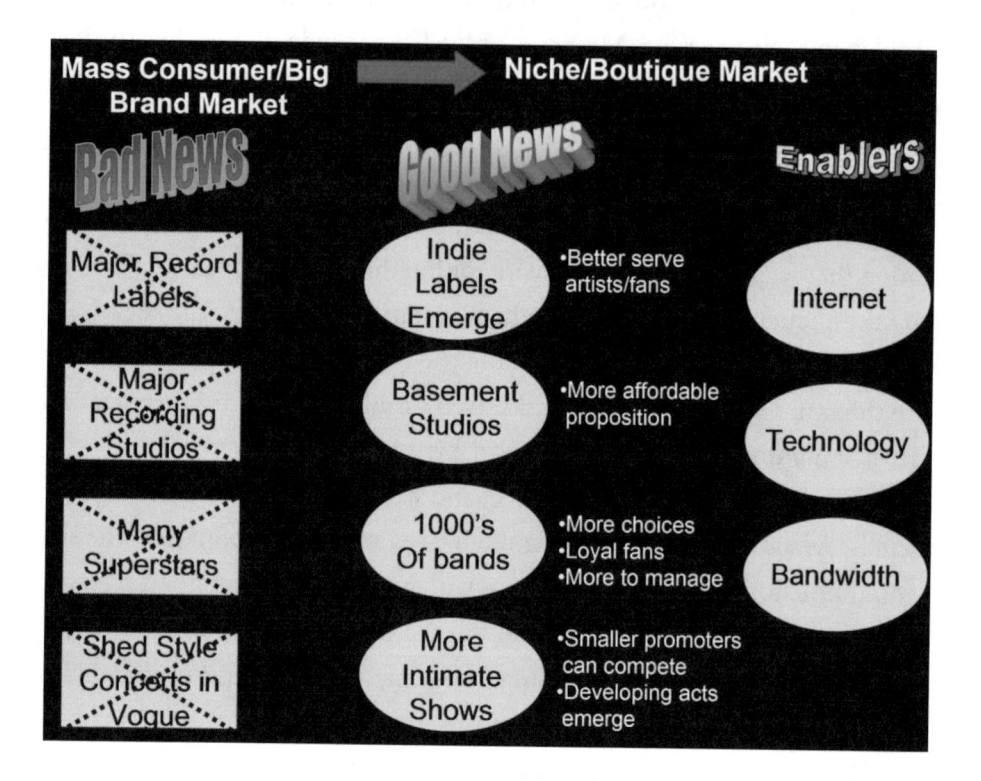

Mass Consumer/Big Brand Market →	Niche/Boutique Market		Enablers
Bad News	**Good News**		
Major Record Labels	Indie Labels Emerge	•Better serve artists/fans	Internet
Major Recording Studios	Basement Studios	•More affordable proposition	Technology
Many Superstars	1000's Of bands	•More choices •Loyal fans •More to manage	Bandwidth
'Shed Style' Concerts in Vogue	More Intimate Shows	•Smaller promoters can compete •Developing acts emerge	

Consequently, I had totally shifted gears by early January 2006 and was ready to go out and fund the new business. Suddenly, my destiny became crystal clear. I was going to be an entrepreneur leading a Web 2.0 startup in the music industry. BandDigs was going to be my ticket to financial independence and a boat-load of fun too. No trips to Asia required!

Below you will find the summary level project timeline for the company as I initially laid it out. You will learn about the gory details in the coming chapters. Strap on your big boy/girl pants! (Green or no X = on time, Yellow or X = 1-6 months late, Red or XX= over 6 months late).

SUMMARY BANDDIGS PROJECT SCHEDULE

Task	Planned Start	Actual Start	Planned End	Actual End
Create business plan	Nov-05	Nov-05	Apr-06	
Build prototype	Jan-06		Feb-06	
Seed funding presentations	Dec-05		Apr-06	
BandDigs site development	Jan-06		Jun-06	
50+ person chat space dev	Jan-06		Jun-06	
Seed round funding	Apr-06		May-06	
Pilot artist events	Apr-06		May-06	
Beta site launch	Jul-06		Jul-06	
Site launch and press release	Sep-06		Sep-06	
Series A funding presentations	Sep-06		May-07	
Series A funding	Jun-07		Jun-07	
Investment bankers engaged	Not planned			
Presentations to acquirers	Not planned			

Chapter 4

WHAT A GREAT IDEA...
LET'S FUND THIS PUPPY!

To secure the funding needed to get the business off the ground, I knew I would need to have a working prototype, and not just rely on pretty PowerPoint slides.

One of my trusted business contacts and best friend for over thirty years led me to an IT development company in Boston, Massachusetts, that he used to work for. The company specialized in video, so they seemed like a great fit. He endorsed their capabilities, so I immediately met with the president of the company. The president assured me his company could build the prototype that I needed to convince others that my idea was sound. In fact, his company had recently built websites for two different organizations that had some of the features I was looking for. One was a professional soccer site and the other was a professional boxing site.

Since I won't have many flattering things to say about this company from here on out, I am going to use false company and employee names to protect the innocent—namely, me. Let's call the development company Inept Solutions, Inc. and its president Phil Johnson.

Here is **LESSON LEARNED #4: When you are going to entrust your entire financial future to an outside vendor** such as Inept Solutions, **do ALL your homework, no matter who recommends them to you.** In my former roles as chief information officer, I had always conducted detailed due diligence on new IT vendors. I did not do so with this vendor and, as you will see, it came back to bite me—frequently—for the next two-plus years. I still lose sleep over this decision. By the way, I don't blame my friend at all for his reference. He knew the company at an earlier time. This was squarely on my shoulders.

At this stage, I needed to step up to pay for the prototype and other startup costs out of my own pocket. Hey, good thing I had that home equity line! It's amazing how easy it is to write those checks. Of course, I was convinced I was investing in a sure thing. The idea was too good for it not to make me millions of dollars, even if it took a few years to materialize. I was living the fantasy of the founders of YouTube and Myspace! Assuming I'd make millions in the end, the return on my investment would be better than anything else I could invest in… right?

Inept Solutions started to work on the prototype at the end of January 2006. They expected it to take four to six weeks to complete. They filmed my daughter Jillian talking with a few "fans" to create the illusion that she was interacting with these kids over the Internet using the BandDigs video chat space.

While this was taking place, I started working on the graphics for the website mockup and the BandDigs logo with Inept. This was not an easy process. Website layouts are like artwork and, as such, emote different feelings from each person. After numerous attempts by Inept to satisfy me, I agreed to this logo.

To further legitimize the logo, I ran it by a bunch of teenagers that my kids knew and about a dozen bands that I knew to see what they thought. They all seemed to be happy with it. I was quite pleased with this, and we immediately began to use the logo in all our documentation. It also drove the overall color scheme/design & layout of the website from that point on.

Little did I know at the time, the graphic of the guy holding the guitar in the background was clip art, readily available to anyone who wanted to make use of it. Even worse, the person who had designed the logo was a contractor, and was not a direct employee of Inept Solutions. When Phil Johnson decided to let the contractor go, the contractor hired an attorney and claimed he had designed the logo and the BandDigs site graphics in general and that it was all his intellectual property. He wanted to be paid a lump sum of money for this work. Yellow Brick Road was served with notice from this contractor's attorney as well, so it got pretty messy. In the end, Yellow Brick Road spent several thousand dollars to resolve this issue between Inept and the contractor.

LESSON LEARNED #5: Validate your copyrights! I should have asked for the designer to document that he/she had really designed the logo upfront before we started to use it and that he/she hadn't used clip art that was generally available to the public. In our case, any other company could have picked the same guitar player graphic, slapped their name on top of it, and used it, which would have caused brand confusion in the marketplace.

I also should have insisted that the designer explicitly waive any rights to the design work and should have asked Inept to assign all rights to Yellow Brick Road as soon as the design was accepted.

Once the contractor issue was behind us, the logo was finalized and Inept Solutions shifted their focus to designing the look and feel of the online community. After a couple of weeks, they provided me with a link to a site layout for my perusal. When I clicked on it, I had expected to be blown away, but instead I was bored out of my damn mind. The first layout looked like a site built for a dentist office—nothing like the many examples of sites that I did like, which had been sent to Inept Solutions in advance. I called Phil Johnson and expressed my displeasure. It was as if they had completely forgotten our intended demographic and our industry. There was absolutely nothing special about what they had designed.

They apologized and went back to the drawing board. A couple of weeks later, they unveiled the design I was looking for. I tested it with my network of contacts, and everyone was pleased with it. This testing approach was the beginning of what would turn out to be our Artist and Fan Pilot program. I will speak to this in more detail in the next chapter, but the basic approach was to have approximately ten artists and ten fans actively involved in the design and testing of the BandDigs site/tools as we built the site.

I have included a screenshot of the prototype chat space below. By the way, at the end of the book, I have provided links to videos that demonstrate the tools, if you're interested in seeing them when they were operational. In fact, you can learn a lot more about the tools and see some other promo videos at www.ybrentertainment.net

The prototype ended up taking about twelve weeks to complete. About halfway through the prototype buildout, I started to line up meetings with potential investors. Even though the prototype wasn't completed, I was able to use parts of it for demos by late February. **LESSON LEARNED #6: If you outsource a project to a vendor who takes twice as long than said vendor had promised to finish a prototype, re-consider giving them the contract for the full development effort.** Seriously, in hindsight I am really perplexed at how patient I was. That was my opportunity to lay down tighter ground rules. I guess because it was early in the relationship, I thought I could whip them into shape. As it would turn out, I totally underestimated the task.

Even though the prototype was delayed, I started to get excited about the prospects of becoming the CEO of a VC-funded Web 2.0 startup. I figured that a technology-based business, with me at the helm, would be hard for the VC firms to ignore. Could this finally be the big break that I had been looking for? Looking back now, I have a hard time believing I was that naïve. **LESSON LEARNED #7: Know the rules when you are playing the game with VCs.** I clearly did not understand how VCs sized up deals. For starters, just because some of them knew me in the context of other high-tech startups, did not mean they would be a fit for me in the music industry. They may have respected me for the work I did with those other companies, but that wouldn't necessarily carry over into an industry where I was quite new. Furthermore, your business model needs to be able to withstand the growth projection test that all VC's will apply to your plan. More on this in lesson #37.

Nonetheless, after the prototype was ready and thoroughly tested, the business plan was refined, and the executive summary was drafted, I was ready to hit the road. I started with my VC contacts at Kodiak Venture Partners—the guys that knew me best, mainly through my work with Ron Borelli at Aavid Thermal Technologies over the years. I figured they wouldn't beat me up too badly, so I would "get my feet wet" with them first.

> Ron was my sure ticket to getting help from Kodiak. Ron had made them a ton of money over the years, and I was doing some consulting work on the side for him at a new venture he was running, Bentley Kinetics. Kodiak was the lead investor in the company. Ron was full of life and a brilliant business guy at seventy years old. He tried to retire a couple times, but opportunities kept calling his name. Unfortunately, about six months into my process, Ron suffered a brain aneurysm and passed away suddenly. Not only did this hurt my chances with Kodiak, this hurt me greatly personally. Here was a man who had worked hard his whole life only to succumb so quickly before he could retire and enjoy the fruits of his labor. I lost my mentor and a good friend that fateful day.

LESSON LEARNED #8: Never start with your BEST funding option. Save them for later, once you've made a few mistakes and have tightened up your pitch. I really should have "practiced" with some individual investors and lower-probability VCs before approaching Kodiak. As I will discuss later, there was quite a bit about the business model that I didn't understand at this early stage of the process. Hence, I'm sure I came across that way to my best contacts right out of the gate. See the appendix for some of the slides I used early on with prospective investors (Exhibit B).

After my first meeting with Kodiak, it became clear to me that I was going to need to talk to some angel investors as well (angel investors are private investors who invest as individuals or as part of a group). Don't get me wrong; the Kodiak guys really liked the prototype and said they wanted to see more before jumping in. They wanted to ensure the business model made sense before investing. Even in this first VC meeting with my best contact, I heard the words "Come back and see us when you can show us the traction." On one hand, this was a little disappointing, but on the other, the doors were not closed . . . or so I thought. How hard could "traction" be, whatever that was?

One specific lesson here worth mentioning: VCs as a standing rule will not say "no." You'll need to read between the lines for yourself. I met with people who knew me when I worked for very successful firms, and as you will see in subsequent chapters, they didn't tell me "no" for over a year. We're all guilty of hearing what we want to hear. Even when they *did* say, "no," I just kept hearing "maybe" and not "Please don't let the door hit you on your way out today." **LESSON LEARNED #9: Not hearing "yes" from a VC means "no thank you."**

After several unsuccessful VC meetings, I decided to research every angel investment group in the Northeast and then approach them one at a time. Fortunately, I had attended a regional angel investor meeting in the fall of 2005 when I was working with Joe Fletcher, so I had several contact names to start with. I also asked my corporate attorney for some referrals. I knew that he had worked with a lot of startups and would have several more contact names for me.

Subsequently, I started off by approaching a very organized angel group called the eCoast Angels located in Portsmouth, New Hampshire, one of the most prominent groups in the New England area. They expressed interest in seeing a demo and hearing my pitch. I first needed to present to a sub-group of investors (like most Angel groups require), and if I passed the test with them, I would be invited to present to the full group at their monthly meeting. One of their leaders was a former Digital Equipment Corporation guy like me, so we had quite a bit in common. By this time, I had the prototype working well enough for a solid demonstration.

The first meeting went according to plan, and they left the door open for me to approach the full group when I felt ready to do so. They had asked a few questions about the business model that I was not able to answer as thoroughly as I felt I should have. Before approaching the larger group, I embarked on a process to address all the questions the sub-group had raised.

In the meantime, I had dinner with a friend of mine in town who was an individual investor. He had made enough money a few years earlier to retire from a successful pharmaceutical-related startup in his early fifties. I wasn't thinking of him as an investor in Yellow Brick Road at the time, but out of force of habit, I gave him my standard elevator pitch on my new venture. I mainly wanted to get his advice on how I might approach potential investors. Much to my surprise, he immediately expressed interest in the business. Not only that, he said he felt he could bring four or five other investors to the table, should I be interested.

It was a whirlwind from that point on. After several meetings and demos with him and his contacts, the investment route looked very promising. In parallel, I met with another friend of mine in town, who was a co-owner of an amusement park and a lifelong musician. He was a former member of a prominent psychedelic Boston-based band back in the '60s that opened for the likes of The Who, Janice Joplin, The Beach Boys, The Blues Project, and Moby Grape. The band had been signed to MGM Records and released two albums that met with some commercial success. He fell in love with the BandDigs concept and offered to invest in the company. Of course, I said, "Welcome aboard!"

All this transpired over forty-five days, and then we were into the legal process of creating the term sheet and the supporting documentation to allow Yellow Brick Road to bring in a group of accredited investors (more on what accredited means in chapter 8). (See Exhibit C) for a copy of the term sheet.

At the end of April 2006, six individual investors had joined in at $100,000 each. After much negotiation, each investor owned 5% of the company, so I had given up 30% of the business to the six investors in the seed round.

We calculated the first round of investment/valuation as follows:

- $1.4 million = Pre-investment valuation (basically the value of the idea, the prototype, the strategic alliances and the design of the site)
- Add their $600,000 investment
- Equaled $2 million post seed round valuation
- $600,000 divided by $2 million = 30% ownership position

Wow, this meant that my shares were worth $1.4 million on paper. Not a bad boost to my balance sheet…

Easy come, easy go as you will find out!

INVESTOR PROFILES

Here is a quick snapshot of each of the Yellow Brick Road investors. Out of respect for their privacy, I will only use numbers when I refer to them:

Investor 1: Retired fifty-four-year old pharmaceutical sales & marketing VP and the catalyst for bringing in four additional investors. Second-time angel investor (invested in a chemical company in the Midwest eight months prior to Yellow Brick Road and occupied a seat on the chemical company's board of directors). Graduated from Brown University. Investor 1 was a VERY likable, gregarious, intelligent, and generous man. He was the type of guy who seemed to know everyone wherever he went. His background was sales & marketing, but almost exclusively in the pharmaceutical industry. He had a passion for music and sports.

Investor 2: Sixty-year-old insurance agency owner/president. Second-time angel investor, invested in a chemical company in the Midwest eight months prior to Yellow Brick Road with Investor 1 and was brought in by Investor 1. Like Investor 1, he had also occupied a seat on the chemical company's board of directors. He had graduated from Columbia University. Investor 2 was extremely intelligent, pragmatic, and personable. He had an excellent reputation in the insurance industry. He wasn't as willing to serve up softballs to me during meetings like some of the other investors. He did ask some pointed questions, especially toward the end of the project. He had limited knowledge about Web 2.0 or the music industry.

Investor 3: Fifty-five-year-old insurance agency owner and real estate investor from Florida. Brought in through Investor 1. Lifelong friend of Investor 1. Investor 3 had a nephew who helped on the project, so he knew a little more about some of our technical struggles as compared to the other investors. He was comfortable allowing Investor 1 to speak for him. I never actually met him in person.

Investor 4: Fifty-three-year-old lawyer out of Florida and brother of Investor 3. First-time angel investor. Brought in by Investor 1. Lifelong friend of Investor 1. Like Investor 3, Investor 4 was the most transparent to me. I only spoke to him a couple of times, and he trusted Investor 1 to represent him. He did attend some of the meetings via phone, but rarely asked questions.

Investor 5: Fifty-four-year-old doctor. First-time angel investor. Brought in through Investor 1. Close friend of Investor 1. This investor was the least tech savvy of the group and even less familiar with the music industry. He was an extremely nice guy and very intelligent, but was somewhat of a fish out of the water on Yellow Brick Road. He trusted Investor 1 to look out for his interests. He did attend all the meetings, but more as an observer.

Investor 6: Fifty-nine-year-old co-owner of a prominent amusement park. First-time angel investor. Former recording artist in the '60s, signed to MGM Records. He didn't know any of the other investors prior to investing in Yellow Brick Road. Investor 6 was very successful in his business. With his background in music/entertainment industry, he added value to some of the discussions. He also knew a few people in the music industry and eventually introduced me to these people. The problem was that his contacts were from a generation ago, so in most cases they just weren't relevant enough to help us.

As you can see, none of these guys were slouches. They were all very successful people in their own professions.

Back to the funding for a minute. The $600,000, plus the cash I had already put in, was projected to carry Yellow Brick Road Entertainment through the full development effort, allow me to pay myself a nominal salary ($100K) and support the hiring of a sales-and-marketing person. The first version of the business plan basically called for us to build the site and generate revenue in the first year by selling subscriptions to the bands, labels, studios, clubs, etc. and advertising on the site. I have provided details from the financial assumptions in the appendix (Exhibit D). Therein, you will see that I had assumed I would raise just $400,000. I'd raised $200K more than that. All the more reason for thinking we were off to a good start!

In early April, the following news story hit the web:

£1m deal for webcam singer
By Richard Simpson, Daily Mail
4 April 2006

Struggling singer Sandi Thom knew she couldn't afford to take her music to the masses.

So with the help of the Internet she got the masses to come to her instead.

Now after 200,000 fans worldwide logged in to nightly concerts in her basement flat, she has signed a £1million record deal.

Record label RCA/Sony BMG signed her up for five albums - in a meeting broadcast live on the Internet yesterday.

The broadcast of her gigs over three weeks last month, Twenty One Nights From Tooting, took her from struggling musician with a handful of admirers to a cyberspace phenomenon.

At first, 70 fans logged in to hear her folk-music gigs, typified by the song I Want to be a Punk Rocker, which ironically bemoans the influence of computers on modern life.

By the twelfth night, however, she had an audience of 182,000 (by comparison, the new Wembley Stadium holds 90,000). They were watching from as far afield as Russia, the U.S. and Pakistan.

'It's been a whirlwind,' Miss Thom, 24, said last night. 'We never realised we'd be in this position just a few weeks after deciding to stick a webcam in the basement.

'We were basically too poor to tour. We brought in so little money thrashing up and down the country in my car - which is a total heap.

'It was so expensive playing to 200 people a night. We thought "Surely there must be another way?"'

Miss Thom and the other three members of her band live in a rented basement flat in a terraced house in Tooting, South London. Their landlord used to be a jazz musician and had kitted out one room as a sound-proofed recording studio.

RCA label director Craig Logan said: 'Sandi is a very talented artist with an already unique story. We're very excited that we're now going to be a part of that story as she develops into a major artist.'

Miss Thom was born in Banff, north east Scotland. Her parents are both helicopter pilots. She started performing at 14 and attended the Institute of Performing Arts in Liverpool.

Her debut album Smile, It Confuses People, will be released on June 5.

Obviously, this added another level of credibility to my business plan. Furthermore, my investors had a second proof point that BandDigs had serious potential. The first point was that Myspace had been acquired by News Corp just a few months prior for $580 million with $0 in revenue.

I used this webcam-singer example in just about every pitch that I gave to bands, labels, managers, and investors from that point on.

The news was exciting, but while it came to light, I was making a very fundamental mistake in my own business planning process. I started believing my own bullshit. I thoroughly convinced myself that I knew what I was talking about. Looking back, this was a flagrant error on my part. Why didn't I take the time to consult with a few industry experts on the details of the business plan? I did meet with quite a few folks about the concept early on, to get their feedback on the BandDigs concept, but unfortunately not on the business/financial model.

LESSON LEARNED #10: Do not write your business plan in a vacuum and DON'T believe your own BS! Make sure you've tested your financial models/logic/assumptions thoroughly with people who know your industry, even if you pay for experts to look at your plan and challenge you on it. Five of my six investors did not have a music industry background.

None of the six offered feedback on the plan whatsoever. They fell unfortunate victims to my charming BS. When I read these ASSumptions now, I cringe! I was living in a dream world and no one called me on it.

LESSON LEARNED #11: When you are creating and organizing your business plan, take time to write a couple different versions. As you will see, we ended up making a major mid course correction less than a year into our plan of record. I really wish I had taken the time in the beginning to build different scenarios—not when we were in the middle of trying to commercialize the product. By then, there just wasn't enough time in the day to deal with it properly.

That point aside, when the checks went into the bank account, I took my wife out to dinner (on my own dime, by the way) and we celebrated. I felt victorious. I was a full-fledged CEO of a startup venture in an industry I really wanted to work in. I had taken an idea in its infancy phase and sold it to six investors, and we were now all poised to make millions of dollars and have fun doing it!

At this point, I really thought my funding work was behind me. My focus would then shift to building the site and generating revenue, both of which I had done many times

> I had left Vette Corp. on Sept 1, 2005, and had not drawn a salary until the investors came on board. I had also invested $40,000 of my own money in the prototype up to that point. If I had stayed at Vette Corp., I would have earned roughly $140,000 (salary and benefits) over that time frame. So, in other words, the opportunity-cost of my idea was already over $180,000. From May onward, I drew a $2,000-per-week salary from Yellow Brick Road Entertainment, which was $90,000 per year *less* than what I was making at Vette. Yeah, but my shares were worth $1.4 million on paper already, so what's the problem? Keep believing the BS, Garry!

before in my thirty-year career. The hard work of funding was behind me, yeehaw! Let's go build a Web 2.0 community that will take the net by storm.

LESSON LEARNED #12: Pay yourself what you are worth. This was another blunder on my part. I looked at the company as "my business" instead of a corporation that I was the majority shareholder in. I worked like a slave for the business for a 50% reduction in salary and benefits from my last job. Don't get me wrong, I did own 70% of the business, so I had an incentive to manage costs and cash flow, but there is absolutely no reason for the CEO of an investor funded startup to take a drastic pay cut while he/she runs the company. If I had been thinking rationally, and hadn't allowed myself to get emotionally caught up in the moment, I would have realized that I needed to raise more capital upfront so that I could afford to pay myself and my employees competitively.

To make matters worse, I decided to locate the business in the basement of my house and pay myself a measly $600 a month in rent until the business started to generate revenue. On the surface, this seemed like a prudent thing to do, but it ended up really disrupting our family life, and it proved inescapable for me each day. Work called my name 24/7, and we had people in and out of the house all day/night long. It also sent the message to all prospects that we met with that we were existing on a shoe string budget. **LESSON LEARNED #13: Find reasonably priced office space near your home that also gives you an identity with your customers and partners.** If you can't afford office space for your startup, you have badly underestimated your funding requirements and are headed for trouble.

During the first round of funding effort, I had turned away a couple of people and had shut down my discussions with the eCoast Angels as soon as the first six people had invested. I didn't want to dilute myself further by bringing more investors on. As it was, I felt that giving up 30% of the business for $600,000 was a lot to part with. **LESSON LEARNED #14: Take the money from investors when you can get it; cash is king! You will spend money faster than your optimistic plan calls for.** Trust me, you can never have enough cash in a startup. You are much better off taking the money in the early stages when you are selling an idea. Once you get further into the process, investors will expect a lot more from you than a business plan and a prototype. After the product is built, you will face much tougher questions and stiffer critiques as you try to commercialize it.

There was an even more important lesson worth mentioning here, which I will cover in more detail in the following chapters. When you are funding a new business and someone offers to write a check as an investor, it is very hard to say "no thank you." One of the biggest mistakes I made was giving away 30% of the company to individuals who could mainly contribute by writing a check.

LESSON LEARNED #15: Bring in investors who can and/or who are interested in doing more for the company than just providing cash. The right investors will help by:

- Providing you with invaluable consulting advice in areas that you are not strong in yourself, e.g. finance, industry perspective, marketing, technology funding process, etc.
- Introducing you to important/influential people in your industry.
- Leading you to the next round of funding through their contacts and experience in raising capital.

I will qualify this by saying it is okay to take "just a check" from a new investor if the majority of your other investors are capable of helping you as I just described. In other words, you should only do so on an exception basis. When you are running a startup like Yellow Brick Road, your investors are really your extended team members. If each of my investors had a background or contacts in my industry, I could have leveraged them regularly over the two-plus years we were together. Instead, after they made their initial investment, I really didn't get much help from them other than a couple of introductions.

Chapter 5

TIME TO HIRE THE TEAM

Here is a quick recap on where we were in March of 2006 on the timeline (just before we closed on the seed-round funding). I have highlighted the task dates below that were started or were completed by the end of March. (Green = on time, Yellow or X = 1-6 months late, Red or XX = over 6 months late).

Task	Planned Start	Actual Start	Planned End	Actual End
Create business plan	Nov-05	Nov-05	Apr-06	
Build prototype	Jan-06	Jan-06	Feb-06 X	Mar-06 X
Seed funding presentations	Dec-05	Dec-05	Apr-06	
BandDigs site development	Jan-06	Jan-06	Jun-06	
50+ person chat space dev	Jan-06	Jan-06	Jun-06	

41

Seed round funding	Apr-06		May-06	
Pilot artist events	Apr-06		May-06	
Beta site launch	Jul-06		Jul-06	
Site launch and press release	Sep-06		Sep-06	
Series A funding presentations	Sep-06		May-07	
Series A funding	Jun-07		Jun-07	
Investment bankers engaged	Not planned			
Presentations to acquirers	Not planned			

Once the prototype was completed, I needed to keep the project moving without the company having the cash in the bank yet to support the project. I was well on my way toward having the funding at this point, but was still working through the details with the investors and lawyers. Of course, I never let the website developers know that Yellow Brick Road wasn't funded yet, as I didn't want to compromise my negotiating position for the full development effort.

Subsequently, I worked with them to develop the detail specs for the site over several weeks, so that they could then provide me with a comprehensive proposal/quote to do the development work. I seriously considered asking some other vendors to submit proposals for the development work, but I was very concerned about the proprietary nature of what we were building. I really thought we had something unique, and did not want anyone else to find out about it until we had it built.

Inept Solutions presented their capabilities to me, including their India operation, which they claimed was created to save their clients money and to speed up their development effort by providing cost-effective around-the-clock development resources.

The president of Inept, Phil Johnson, claimed that the India team was part of his staff, but as I found out months later, the team was really part of his cousin's company and did not actually work for him. This proved to be a serious issue for us during the project. Can you spell *due diligence*?

When Phil presented his proposal to me, I knew it was a very aggressive plan, but since he had shown me a fair amount of the work already completed for other clients, that could be leveraged for us, I was reluctant to challenge him too much. I was also blinded a bit by what I felt was a fair price. Lastly, I let myself hear what I wanted to hear. Phil presented me with a project plan, resource model, and the formal technical specs. What more could I ask for?

Back to **LESSON LEARNED #4** for a moment. **When you are going to entrust your entire financial future to an outside vendor, do your homework, no matter who recommends them to you.** Remember, one of my closest and trusted friends referred me to Inept, having worked for them in the past. That said, one of the bigger mistakes I made was not asking Phil for customer references and then checking them. I am positive I would have found out that Inept had a track record of over-promising and not delivering projects on time. Well, just a few weeks into the BandDigs project, I discovered just how "inept" Inept Solutions really was.

I shared the full proposal from Inept with the Yellow Brick Road attorney, and we proposed a specific website development agreement that more clearly defined the deliverables, specifications, IP ownership, copyrights, schedule, and pricing. It took several weeks of back-and-forth negotiation between attorneys before we had the contract nailed down. We operated on a handshake basis in the meantime, so that we could keep the project rolling. I had to advance $28,500 to officially launch the project. I would then have a month or so before the next payment would be due if Inept was on schedule. Out came the home-equity-line checkbook! I invested the money into Yellow Brick Road, and Yellow Brick Road wrote the check to Inept Solutions Inc. Something that later paid off for me from a tax standpoint as I will discuss in Lesson #42.

The prototype work laid the foundation for the eventual site/tools design. We had already created the look and feel for the site, the layout, and the basic navigation. Check out the appendix (Exhibit E) for the Banddigs Deliverables list.

The project launch date was April 17, 2006, and the anticipated "go live" date was June 23, 2006. In other words, the BandDigs site was supposed to be built, tested, and launched in just nine weeks, leveraging what Inept Solutions had supposedly built for other clients in some form or fashion.

I figured that, based on this schedule, I could safely commit September 1, 2006 for the site launch, to my investors. Even if Inept was off by 100%, I thought that they could surely complete the site by Labor Day. Little did I know how far off the mark they would end up being.

LESSON LEARNED #16: When you get a schedule from your outside developer, demand to see the details, including resource loading/hours, etc. Ask them to show you their contingency plan in case the project starts to slip. Also, insist that a project manager is assigned to manage all the details of your project. DO NOT trust your vendors to deliver the project on time without supervising their every move. You may even want to negotiate for one of your staff to have an office onsite next to their project manager. **LESSON LEARNED #17: Include a bonus clause in the contract with your vendors for work done on time or a penalty clause for work delivered late.** As it turned out, BandDigs was not launched until December 1, 2006, and it was launched in beta mode without the most important feature, the 50+ person video chat space with the recording capability. In other words, the basic functionality was delivered over five months late and other key features were delivered almost a year late (some were NEVER delivered). More on this to come…

Throughout the funding process, I knew I would need to hire a senior, industry-savvy sales & marketing person to help me network to more labels, artists, and music-related businesses and to begin to sell our subscription services and our advertising as soon as the site was built and launched. I began to plant this seed with my contacts, and a few candidates emerged during the next couple of months.

At the end of the summer of 2006, I made the decision to bring in a sales & marketing manager to help me. The person I hired had been Al Kooper's (Blood, Sweat and Tears) personal assistant in the past. A quick aside; did you know that Al played the organ on "Like a Rolling Stone" for Bob Dylan and co-wrote the song "This Diamond Ring" for Gary Lewis and the Playboys? The candidate had also handled local music promotion for the largest New Hampshire radio station, and had recently spent a year or so working for an Internet radio station. She came recommended by a band member from my Granite Rocks Records days, whom I knew very well.

By this point, I was working late seven days a week and didn't have a whole lot of time to spend on searching for candidates, so I justified hiring her based on this one recommendation. I had only interviewed a couple of other candidates, and they were out of my price range, so I selected her for the position.

This position was critical, and yet I didn't even ask her for references. The fact that I only had to pay her $40K a year should have also been a sign that I was talking to the wrong person for the director of sales & marketing position. Don't get me wrong, she was worth the $40K, but she was just not the right fit for the sales & marketing role. I justified hiring her thinking I could have her help me get things started, and then, when we raised more money, I would hire a more senior person to take over. Unfortunately, she didn't have the contacts or the sales experience to make any real impact on the growth of BandDigs. She was however, very comfortable testing the site, reporting the issues, and complaining about Inept.

The problem was that once she had spoken to the twenty or so bands that she knew in the Boston area, she had exhausted her sales and marketing capabilities. She did help me by taking the tools into a few local clubs to do live Internet video broadcasts, but that wasn't enough. **LESSON LEARNED #18: DO NOT settle for someone that you can "afford" for a critical role.** You need to find the very best person for the job and then figure out how to pay the person what he/she deserves and/or offer a lower salary along with a piece of the company.

Realizing I was far from being an expert in the music industry myself, and my investors knew even less about it than I did, I decided to approach a few people to try to form an advisory board of experts. The first few people I spoke to asked me for a piece of the company in return for their services. I told them I'd think about it and would get back to them, but I never followed through with it. I had even gone as far as putting together proposals to two different advisors with our attorney's help, but *didn't follow through*. **LESSON LEARNED #19: If you want people to help you, be prepared to give them a share of the company in return.**

I was worried about diluting myself by bringing these industry folks onboard. I should have structured the deals in such a way that they would have earned their shares by helping me open doors to funding, partners, etc. over time. This was a major missed opportunity. It was the one place I might have been able to get some help from an extended team.

That said, six months after I had hired the sales & marketing manager, I hired a part-time sales & marketing consultant, Richard Ellis, who brought a lot to the table. Richard had over 20 years of experience in the entertainment industry, holding executive positions at **Warner Music Group, Sony Music, BMG, Time Inc, Musician Magazine and Contemporary Productions.** He was one of the people whom I had initially approached about being on Yellow Brick Road's advisory board. Joe Fletcher from my concert promoting days had introduced me to him.

Richard opened doors for me at Geffen/A&M, Disney, Rounder Records, Digital Media Wire, Windup Records, etc. Since I was paying him as a consultant, I really didn't feel that I should also have to compensate him as an advisor, so I held off executing a broader agreement. The trouble was that he was not nearly as motivated to help me as he would have been if he was into the company for equity.

While wrestling with the idea of bringing on compensated advisors, I did reach out to several people that I knew in the business who I thought would be beneficial to have a strategic alliance with. Some of these people in effect would also become uncompensated advisors. They were three CEOs of successful music-related businesses in the Boston area (CD manufacturing, artist management and marketing). They were all folks that I met with regularly to share war stories and discuss ways to help each other.

In the end, despite working on many such alliances, none of them produced any material results. We wasted a lot of time trying to figure out synergies and ways to co-promote that in the end contributed very little to our registration rate. **LESSON LEARNED #20: Do not count on alliances to do your marketing and/or to bring you any new customers.** If you decide to invest time in any strategic alliances, make sure you each have specific goals and ways to measure whether the alliance is working. If you don't see any results after a few months, forget the relationship and move on.

Chapter 6

READY TO LAUNCH...
THROW ME A LIFE JACKET

As I mentioned earlier in the book, I used an Artist and Fan Pilot program to provide us with a check-and-balance for our design efforts. The last thing I wanted to build was a site that no one in our targeted demographic liked or could work with. My connections from Granite Rocks Records and from managing my daughter came in handy at this point. I could pick up the phone and arrange to work with a myriad of signed/unsigned bands and music businesses. The bands were on labels such as Motown, RCA, and Columbia. Our pilot-program terms are listed at the back of the book in Exhibit F.

In addition to these pilot artists, Investor 3's nephew (and one of our fan pilot members) had an A&R contact at Virgin Records, Don Rohr, who would turn out to be a great supporter. The nephew also knew a few managers that he introduced me to.

Our pilot artists had a total of 500,000+ Myspace friends (registered users) on their Myspace pages! Even if 20% of their fans signed up for

BandDigs, we'd have 100,000 fans on the site virtually overnight. The basic idea was for each band to virally market the site to their fan base. In fact, we provided each band with a graphic that could be posted to their website and/or Myspace page that would provide a direct link to their page on BandDigs.

One of the more uplifting moments for me was when Don Rohr in New York invited me down to his office to pitch BandDigs to the whole A&R and Digital Media Department at Virgin Records. I had been to Elektra Records in New York City a couple years before with Jillian, so I had a taste for what it might be like to meet with a big label, but this was my first time pitching BandDigs to one of the "big guys" in the industry.

I was a little worried about presenting the concept/prototype at this early stage, so I asked for a mutual nondisclosure agreement to be signed in advance of the meeting. Don wasn't sure if he could make that happen, but he told me that he would try to take care of it before my arrival.

When I showed up for the meeting after a five-plus hour drive, Don told me he was unable to get the document signed internally, so I had a choice to make. I could either take the risk of sharing our prototype to an audience of approximately twenty people who controlled many bands with very large fan bases, or I could leave and face the prospect of never being invited back to Virgin again. I decided to roll the dice and share what I brought with me.

As a result of the meeting, we added several bands to our pilot program. In total, the bands would bring an additional 100,000 Myspace friends with them. Moreover, we captured Virgin's interest overall. They absolutely loved the concept. In fact, Don Rohr recapped what he saw at the end of the meeting by saying, "BandDigs is going to be fucking huge!" This, of course, gave me immediate heart palpitations, reinforcing everything I had hoped to hear. We could be the next Myspace, man. I would be happy to sell BandDigs a few years down the road for the same $580 million that Myspace brought in, and I was sure my investors would be ecstatic with that type of return.

So, up to this point in the timeline (June of 2006), the Yellow Brick Road extended team included the following members:

- President/CEO (my role)
- Sales & marketing manager
- Sales & marketing industry consultant (part-time)
- 6 outside investors
- Inept Solutions (developers)
- Corporate attorney
- Patent attorney
- Licensing attorney (site terms, song & video licensing, etc.)
- 3 uncompensated industry CEO's
- Corporate accountant
- 15 pilot artists/music businesses
- 10 pilot fans/interns

So, the team at least appeared to be fairly robust by this point. Bear in mind, as I hired people and continued to meet with leads, referrals, bands, etc., I also continued to drive Inept to complete the site work. This was a full-time job for me for many months. Inept assigned a project manager, who only lasted a few weeks before she left the company (probably because she knew she couldn't be successful). I held weekly project review meetings with Phil Johnson and a couple of his people, but frankly, this was not nearly enough. In hindsight, I should have spent two or three days a week at Inept's offices until they fixed the project manager issue. I created a bug-tracking report and provided daily/weekly reports to Inept of all the open bugs. Since they weren't doing it, I'd decided to take the bull by the horns.

Not unexpectedly, the planned project completion date of June 23 came and went, and Inept wasn't remotely close to finishing the site, despite my constant hounding. Week after week, they continued to miss their due dates and/or provided us with inferior work and lame excuses. The bug list grew to hundreds of items. Their India team was an absolute joke. They couldn't do anything right, and they never tested the changes that they made. To make matters worse, they had no controls around code releases. They just dropped things onto the equivalent of our production server, which totally hosed the site overnight for us to clean up the next morning when we came in.

You are probably wondering why in the world I didn't fire them. Believe me, not a day passed when I didn't think of doing just that. Here is the rub. If I fired Inept, it would mean starting over with another vendor. These guys had already developed the prototype and supposedly had the chat space and webcast tools that were needed partially developed. Above all, we could not afford to lose the time. And primarily, we couldn't afford to start over with another vendor financially without more cash.

So, I was stuck in a totally dysfunctional relationship! I lost all trust in Inept to do anything on time or to do it correctly. I even adopted the routine of meeting Phil Johnson every Sunday morning for breakfast to recap the issues of that week—to essentially plead for more support.

As functionality was delivered by Inept, albeit late, I had six interns who helped test the features and provided feedback as it came together. We also had several of our pilot artists work with the site. This testing served two purposes: 1) we discovered bugs faster, and 2) we received feedback on the site features and ease of use. I highly recommend this approach.

This is where the sales & marketing manager spent most of her time, testing the site and working with the interns and bands. It was important work, but while she focused on the testing she did not spend time on business development.

By September we were finally ready to do some live video broadcasts to test out the experience with real fans of a few of the pilot artists. This was very fun. We rented a rehearsal space in Boston called Jamspot and had bands perform live while we invited their fans to watch the show on their computers at home. We sent the fans a link via email. They clicked on the link, and up popped a BandDigs window where the video was displayed. It was like a live version of YouTube. Here is an example of what the Webcast tool looked like:

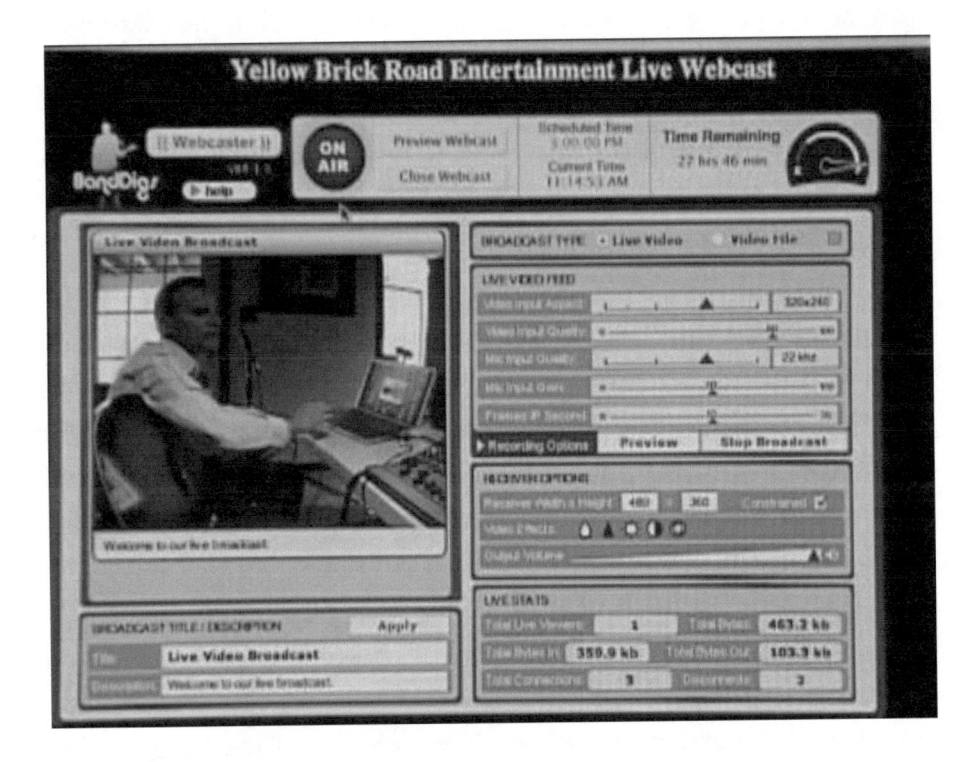

We ran three different broadcasts over a four-week period and then collected feedback from the fans to see what they liked and what they didn't like about the experience. One of the ideas we added was a text box that fans could use to send questions to the band during the broadcast.

Inept was so far behind schedule that they proposed launching BandDigs with a smaller video chat application (up to ten people in the chat room with the band) instead of the 50+ that I had specified and had promoted to everyone that we had been dealing with. We didn't really have a choice. If we were going to launch the site before someone else beat us to the punch, we needed to settle for this solution. I acquiesced to keep the project rolling—we needed to get to the market—but I also let them know I was not happy with it.

Consequently, we began testing the ten-person video chat space. It was a far cry from the 50+ person chat space that I had designed, but it gave us something to demonstrate to bands and to investors. The chat space not only allowed up to ten fans to talk to a band, but the band could ask survey questions and have the results displayed on screen. They could also allow fans to send them text questions, however the bands were unable to record the video chats and offer fans a copy of them. Although Inept had promised this feature by the end of the summer, they did not deliver it, nor would they for almost another year!

To me, the 50+ person chat space with recording capability was THE reason for BandDigs. Bands with a fan base would need the bigger chat space with the recording capability to justify spending the time hosting chats on BandDigs. Here was another screw up on my part. **LESSON LEARNED #21: Clearly understand your IP ownership position and ensure that it is well documented between your company and your vendors.** I should have done two things at this point: 1) Had my lawyer draft a letter for the files documenting this temporary solution along with my dissatisfaction, and more importantly, 2) Asked Inept to declare where the chat space came from and whether they owned the IP.

Here is the reason why. About six months later, I was introduced to a company in Connecticut by Richard Ellis that expressed serious interest in potentially acquiring or investing in Yellow Brick Road. This company provided web solutions to almost 3,000 radio stations across the country. They saw BandDigs as a way for stations to provide a level of interaction between DJs, fans, and guests on the radio programs. My meeting and demo was one of the best ones that I'd had with anyone to date. They were salivating when I showed them the capabilities of the site.

I explained that the current chat space was a temporary solution until the new 50+ person chat space was finished. About a week later, I got a call from the president of the interested company. He wanted to know if Yellow Brick Road owned all the intellectual property on the BandDigs site, including the chat space.

I said "yes," really believing that we *did* own the rights to it, at least through our contract with Inept. Little did I know that the ten-person chat space was actually owned by Userplane, an AOL company. Inept had apparently licensed the chat space and integrated it into the BandDigs community, but didn't bother to tell me that they hadn't developed it themselves. It was all legal, as Inept was paying Userplane to license the use of it, but this raised a red flag to the interested company.

Subsequently, the president accused me of being less than honest, and looking back, I was, although I didn't know it at the time. Of course, when he challenged me, I felt as though he had questioned my integrity, so I told him to go screw himself. Bottom line: this cost me a HUGE opportunity. Had I done my homework ahead of time and had Inept been upfront with me, I may have been able to salvage the deal.

LESSON LEARNED #22: Don't take pushback from potential investors and/or acquirers too personally. What I should have done, instead of telling the president of the interested company off, was to say, "I'm sorry for the confusion on this. Let me check into it and get back to you." At that point, I may have been able to explain the issue away and point them back to the 50+ person chat space that was in development. I should have put myself in the interested party's shoes versus getting all caught up in protecting my own integrity.

10-Person Video Chat Space Licensed from Userplane, with our own add on Flash features at the top of the screen (questions and polling)

Allow me to re-visit our tests of the live broadcasts at the rehearsal space for a moment. They proved to be invaluable. We had fifty to one hundred people watching each of the shows, and then we asked for their feedback after the events. The bands really enjoyed the process, and all expressed excitement for using the technology on their own. The feedback continued to validate that we were on the right track. Don't get me wrong; the fans had their issues with the experience, but we felt confident we could address the technical issues. We didn't get discouraged. The main take away for me was that the fans and bands loved the concept and were interested in continuing to use the technology.

While we tweaked the chat space and the video broadcast tool, we worked on the rest of the website. Even though Inept did the actual programming, I provided the direction on the site specs, and my team tested and reported issues to Inept on a daily basis. The BandDigs community was comprised of many features, including the personalization sections for bands, fans, and corporations. This is where a registered user could create their own identity on the site and where the chat space and broadcast tools could be accessed.

Each user could design a custom flash box that included pics and graphics, upload photos, songs and video clips, and blog with others. We even offered a video blog, where bands could quickly record a video using their webcam, post it, and send it to their fans. Fans could also post their own video blog messages on their pages and share them with friends and with the bands they supported.

For band and company subscribers, we offered additional features, such as using the chat space as a host and being able to broadcast live shows, store videos and songs to be sold in the BandDigs download store, record and sell video chat clips, manage fan email lists, etc.

In other words, the site was *very* robust, and some of the features were breakthroughs at the time.

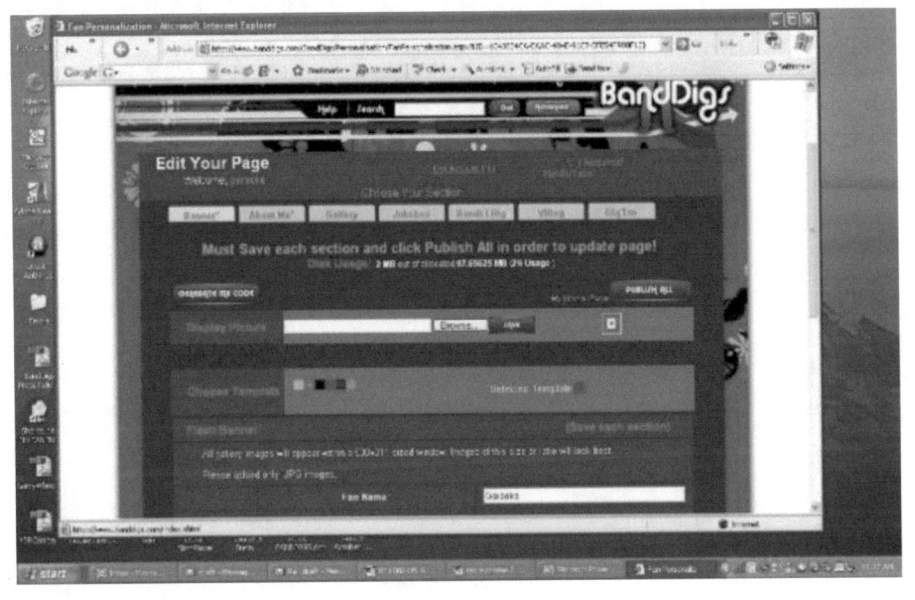

Fan Personalization

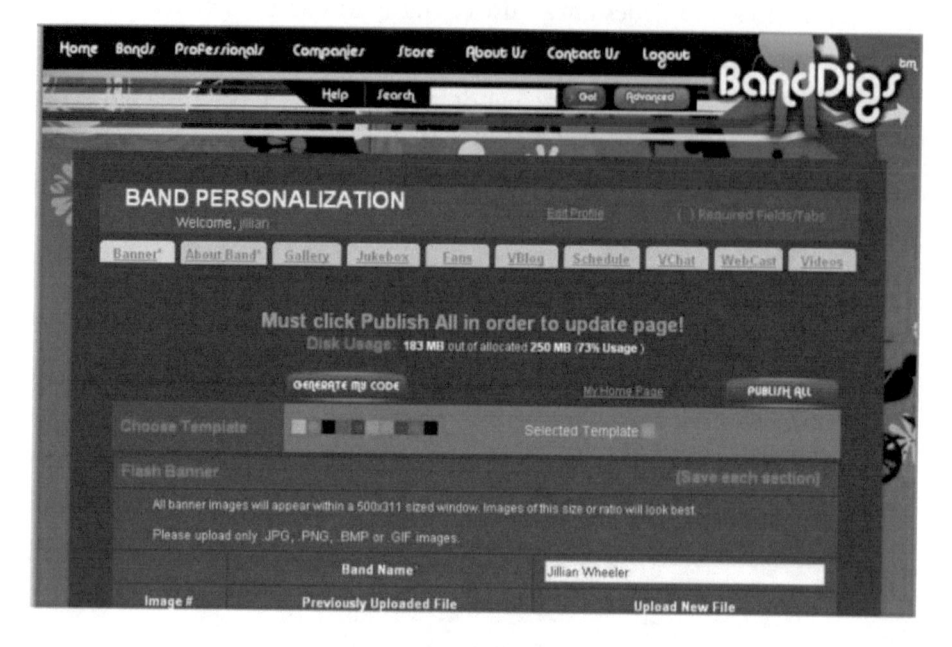

Band Personalization

FROM FAILURE TO FORTUNE 59

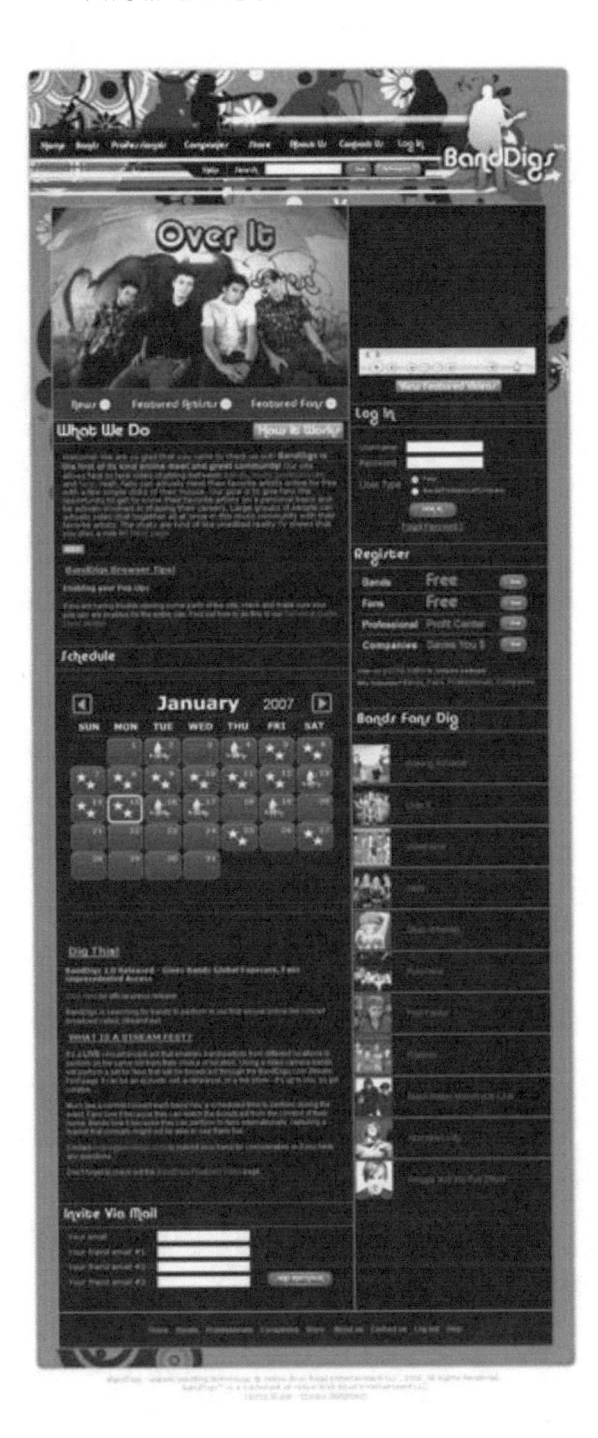

Home Page

BandDigs Platform

Fan Page Example

FROM FAILURE TO FORTUNE 61

Band Page Example

Corporate/Company Page Example

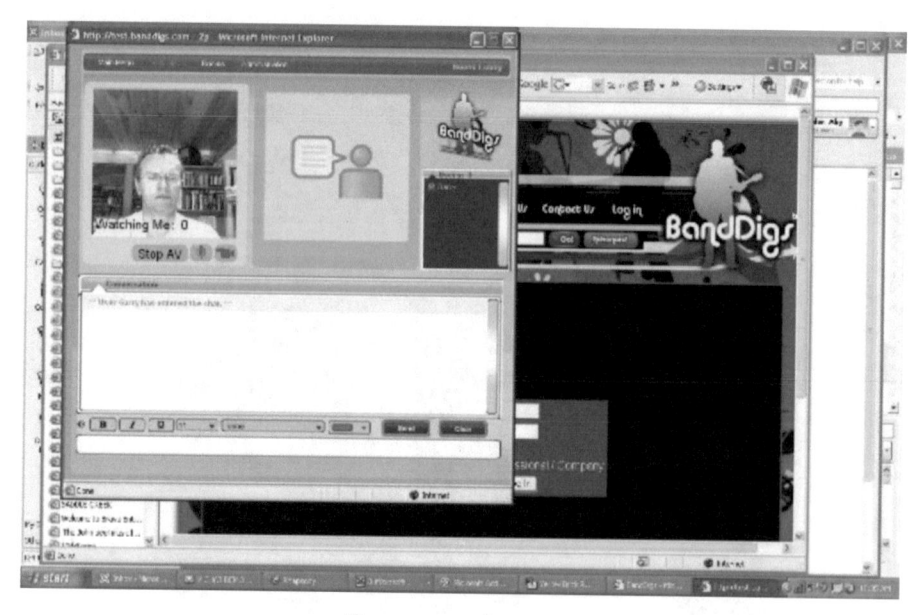

One-on-one chat space

As you can see by the prior screenshots, this was not a trivial project, and I have just scratched the surface of what we created. As we introduced new tools and features, we continued to ask our pilot artists and pilot fans/interns to give us feedback.

To suggest that this was a smooth process would be stretching the truth. Every time we tested, we discovered tons of problems with the site. I could write an entire book on the bugs and problems we found and the issues we had with Inept, but it is water under the bridge and not helpful information for you.

~ ~ ~

We had to chase our pilot artists almost as much as we chased Inept. We'd call them and/or email them to ask for their help and 90% of the time we came up dry. I discovered one very important fact that was reinforced time and time again throughout the project. Musicians just want to play music. **LESSON LEARNED #23: REALLY Know your customers!** This again showed just how naïve I was to the music industry. I went into this project thinking bands would really want to use our tools to build their fan base and to entertain their fans in a way that hadn't been done before. I made a very fundamental mistake here. I figured since I had been willing to work hard at promoting my daughter's music career, that bands in general would be willing to do the same. Man, was I off the mark.

Our real customers were the fans, as it turned out. We needed fans even more than the bands to prove the model and to show the "traction." Initially we thought we needed thousands of bands on the site to pay us a subscription fee, but really what we needed was 100 big-name artists who had a large and passionate fan base. In fact, the local bands meant nothing to the site. If we really knew our potential customers, we would have gone after the big-name artists first.

Perhaps we should have even offered the bigger artists a share in BandDigs if they could have attracted a certain number of fans to the site and agreed to do a monthly event with them on BandDigs. We lost sight of the fact that not all bands or fans were created equal. The fans who would eventually enjoy BandDigs, for example, were the crazed and passionate fans, not the casual fans.

There was another related critical lesson here that would go on to cause us many issues as the project rolled on. We thought MORE functionality on the site was a good thing. We figured if we provided more features, bands would surely want to use them. Instead, the more we added, the more complex the site became. This meant that to take advantage of all the tools, a band would need to invest more time in learning how to use them. Big mistake on our part. We totally missed the mark with our customer base. We should have introduced the bare bones community with the basic chat space and broadcast tools and launched it as quickly as possible to get market feedback.

LESSON LEARNED #24: Get your product to market as quickly as possible, and test it with your customers as you go along. Do not ASSume you know what your customer really wants. In other words, don't speak for your customer. Had we launched sooner and better accommodated our customer, we would have saved money on developing features we didn't need and generated industry buzz earlier.

In our case, we probably would have discovered that we were chasing the wrong customer earlier. As we eventually learned, bands that had managers used the site much more than bands that did not have managers. Managers pushed their bands to use new tools like BandDigs, and they also helped their bands get their content onto the site. The managers saw the value of sites like BandDigs and were not intimidated by them.

Our development efforts continued for months. After beating Inept over the head every week since they'd missed their original launch commitment in June, they finally committed to a launch date of December 1, 2006.

Aren't you wondering what my investors were thinking by now? Well, to keep my investors informed, I set up regular meetings every six weeks to provide them with a formal update on our progress. I also emailed them an update every two or three weeks with a formal status report. By October, it was getting embarrassing for me that we still weren't even close to launching the site.

Consequently, I didn't look forward to the meetings with the investors at all. It was a humbling experience. Every one of them was patient with me and seemed supportive, even though Inept continued to miss their deadlines. In reality, my investors were *too* patient with me. What I really needed were industry experts who could challenge my thinking and help me to solve some of the issues that we continued to struggle with.

LESSON LEARNED #25: Don't surround yourself with passive investors. On the surface, it probably seems great that my investors were so patient and supportive with me. What I could have benefited from, however, was for my investors to push back harder on the schedule, to ask me to explain why we were developing certain features, and to help me access key contacts in the music industry. Our early meetings were more like a club gathering.

My investors were enamored by the technology and the thought that they could make millions of dollars from BandDigs. I was happy to wow them with the latest features on the wide-screen monitor and explain the cool things still being worked on. What can I say? It stroked my ego and creating something new like BandDigs was just plain fun.

While we slowly proceeded down the path, some additional good news hit the press. On October 10, 2006, Google announced its acquisition of YouTube for $1.65 billion. Are you kidding me? Wow! Yet another reason to keep plowing ahead! YouTube had launched about a year and half prior to being acquired. When they were acquired, they had 72 million visitors to their site each month, but had yet to generate any meaningful revenue. Google bought them for their traffic and the potential upside of monetizing the site.

Whatever the reason for the Google deal happening, my investors got VERY excited. I heard from several of them after the announcement, reiterating their belief in BandDigs and what we were about to launch. I must admit, even I started to get more excited about the prospects, thinking that our site had many additional features. I figured it would surely attract a large audience once the bands had spread the word to their Myspace friends.

At my November meeting with the investors, we decided to revisit our revenue model in light of the YouTube deal. We assumed that our exit plan would mean being acquired. After learning that Myspace and YouTube were acquired for a multiple of their user base and not a multiple of revenue, we decided our real objective would be to attract millions of registered users to BandDigs.

Hence, we decided to forgo charging the bands a subscription fee to use the tools on BandDigs. We didn't want to deter bands from joining and inviting their fans to partake in all the fun on the site. We saw this as a major decision for us at the time. I was totally convinced that bands would invite thousands of fans to join BandDigs within thirty days after we launched the site. My sales & marketing manager and I had mapped out a whole series of marketing ideas and planned to equip each band with a viral marketing kit to spread the word about the site.

I had designed in easy linkages to and from Myspace and YouTube so that the bands could easily move content around and could communicate with their fan base more efficiently. Or so I thought.

LESSON LEARNED #26: When you make a major change to your business model, take the time to contemplate the potential consequences. Remember, my original business plan called for us to be generating revenue by September 1, 2006. Not only did that *not* happen due to the site not being ready, we had just pulled the plug on the only real revenue stream that we had in our plan for the first year. If we had taken the time to really consider the implications of that decision, we would have recognized the need to raise additional capital right then. We could have started the process of raising the next round of funding sooner, even if it was from other individual investors. We seemed to lose track of this when we convinced ourselves that we were only eighteen months away from pay dirt—we would surely be the next YouTube deal.

LESSON LEARNED #27: Don't get caught up in the hype of other company's successes—or failures, for that matter. Stay focused on your own business and funding models. Sure, it's a good idea to keep tabs on what is going on in your industry, but your venture needs to stand on its own two feet. You cannot draw any conclusions from what is happening around you. Emotions can definitely take over if you let them. It's your job as an entrepreneur to tune out all the distractions.

The bottom line was that we needed to finish building and testing the damn site so that we could launch it and start creating a massive audience of fans!

Chapter 7

STARTING STRONG, SORT OF

Okay, by the fall of 2006, we finally could see the light at the end of the tunnel. We were gearing up to launch BandDigs on December 1st. Inept Solutions continued to be inept, but I felt that by then, we would have enough developed, tested, and stabilized to open the site for business.

Here is an update on the timeline. Again, I have highlighted the task dates of items started or completed by then. (Green = on time, Yellow or X = 1-6 months late, Red or XX = over 6 months late).

Task	Planned Start	Actual Start	Planned End	Actual End
Create business plan	Nov-05	Nov-05	Apr-06	Apr-06
Build prototype	Jan-06	Jan-06	Feb-06 X	Mar-06 X
Seed funding presentations	Dec-05	Dec-05	Apr-06	Apr-06
BandDigs site development	Jan-06	Jan-06	Jun-06 X	

67

50+ person chat space dev	Jan-06	Jan-06	Jun-06 X	
Seed round funding	Apr-06	Apr-06	May-06	May-06
Pilot artist events	Apr-06 X	Aug-06 X	May-06 X	Oct-06 X
Beta site launch	Jul-06 X	Dec-06 X	Sep-06 X	
Site launch and press release	Sep-06 X	Jan-07 X	Sep-06 X	
Series A funding presentations	Sep-06	Sep-06	May-07	
Series A funding	Jun-07		Jun-07	
Investment bankers engaged	Not planned			
Presentations to acquirers	Not planned			

During our final prep, we informed our artists about the launch date. Yellow Brick Road's interns created pages for all of our pilot artists, businesses, and fans, so that when the site went live, it would at least have some content on it to give new bands and fans a feel for what the site would look like.

We also provided our pilot artists with their viral marketing tools, including animated gifs they could post on their websites and Myspace pages that would redirect their fans and friends to their pages on Band-Digs. My sales & marketing manager and I prepared a press release. We then developed a list of a few hundred bands that she and I knew to send promotional materials to. Everything appeared to be ready for launch.

While finalizing the development, I worked with Yellow Brick Road's patent attorney to start to pull all the materials needed to file our patent application. This was time consuming and expensive, but we figured that having "patent pending" status when we launched would help us with our next round of funding. I have to say, I was unimpressed by the US patent office and related processes. How can a technology-based country expect companies to file for patents blindly and then wait up to seven years for action? It was a ridiculous and worthless exercise from the perspective of protecting our ideas. If you are considering going through this process, I'd strongly suggest you think twice about it.

Since most of the development was being done by leveraging existing tools and technology, the only patent that we could qualify for was a "process & methods patent." So, basically, we were trying to patent how BandDigs was using these tools to provide the overall user experience.

We had to document our processes and tools in great detail to gain patent pending status. Here is an example of just one of the processes:

Live Chat/Broadcast Process

Step 1	Step 2	Step 3
Band Registers event & creates fan invitation	Band invites fans to attend chat (2 way) or broadcast (1 way)	Fans register to attend and pay or redeem points for premium services
Event then shows on group calendar/schedule	Fans click on URL in invitation to join the event	Host tells system to record the event or not
Fans see welcome video and watch ads until host joins	Host joins and event begins (recording starts automatically if selected)	Fans raise hand to ask questions if event is 2 way
Artist opens the fans' webcam image to allow question and answers it	System scrolls the images displayed on screen unless a fan pays to lock it in	Bands ask polling questions and fans respond by clicking mouse
Fans send private text messages to host	Band ends public chat and starts one on one private chats if fans have paid for them	Event concludes, system encodes recorded video and posts it to the chat page for immediate download

Figure 14

Yellow Brick Road spent over $10,000 to submit its first patent application, which then gave us "patent pending" status. As soon as the patent application was accepted, we prominently displayed "patent pending" on all pages of the website and all investor documentation. "Patent pending" status would hopefully give us more credibility with potential investors at least.

In parallel, Investor 2 introduced me to the CEO of a $2 billion apparel company, Aeropostale, with over 700 stores nationally. They were interested in seeing a demo of the site's capabilities, thinking that they might want to deploy our technology throughout their retail stores for live shows and fan interaction. This was our biggest opportunity to date. I got to pitch the BandDigs' platform to the CEO, Julian Geiger, and his executive staff at an offsite meeting.

After my demo, the chief marketing officer asked me straight out, "Why shouldn't we just acquire your company?" I played it cool and said that it was probably a little too early for us to be acquired, but reiterated how excited we would be to work with Aeropostale (looking to gain some traction to boost our price for the company of course).

> Imagine being invited to an offsite meeting like this in my position. I could barely sleep the night before going to the meeting, thinking of all the possibilities. I spent several days tailoring a great demo to Aeropostale's demographic that I planned to show to Julian and his team on a big screen. So, I packed up my laptop, my projector, a stereo system, etc., and headed off to their meeting place. It was on Plum Island in Newburyport, Massachusetts, about an hour from my home. I walked into their meeting room, only to find that it was on the top floor of the building, overlooking the ocean with skylights and glass surrounding the entire room (not a shade, wall, or projector screen in sight). It couldn't have been a brighter meeting room if it was located on the sun! Fortunately, while I was there, a massive thunderstorm blew in and darkened the room a bit (in between flashes of lightning at least). I had everyone gather around my 15-inch laptop, connected my sound system to it, and braved my way through the demo. It worked, but man, it was a scary session.

I could barely contain my excitement during the meeting. It was one huge adrenalin rush! Julian assigned his chief marketing officer to arrange for his team to meet with me once he got back to his office in New York City. He wanted us to figure out the next steps for Aerpostale to leverage BandDigs' capabilities in their stores. Once the details were sorted out, we were all supposed to regroup to discuss our proposed plan.

A few weeks later, I traveled to New York City to meet with one of Aeropostale's vice presidents to explore ways of working together, but with several management changes taking place at the apparel company, I was unable to capitalize on the opportunity. The vice president that I was assigned to work with just didn't get it and had too many competing priorities to spend time with me. To make matters worse, the chief marketing officer, who was the most vocal at the offsite meeting, had abruptly left the company under less than stellar circumstances.

Unfortunately, all this led to us being told "no thank you." I tried to salvage something by asking them to consider running some banner ads on our site and/or running video ads in front of band events, but they wanted to see user numbers, site stats, etc. before committing to spend money with us. The good news was the door was left partially open. "Come back and see us later, Garry."

In the meantime, I had reached out to the booking agent for Teddy Geiger, an up-and-coming seventeen-year-old artist and teen heartthrob. I felt that he would be a perfect fit for BandDigs. His fan base was made up of thousands of teenage girls. The agent connected me to Stealth Management, Teddy's management company. Stealth was owned by Billy Mann, a very successful producer and songwriter who worked with Sting, the Backstreet Boys, Jessica Simpson, Pink, Joss Stone, Ricky Martin and others.

After a couple of phone calls, Billy invited me down to meet with him at his home studio in Connecticut. I successfully demonstrated the video chat space and the broadcast tools along with the interactive features.

Billy loved the site. One of Billy's key guys, Nick Bolton, said, "BandDigs is going to be the next big thing!" They agreed to talk to Teddy about the site, and Billy agreed to consider an offer to become a strategic advisor for Yellow Brick Road. I was on cloud nine after the meeting. This guy was well connected and he knew the business inside and out. He was even mildly interested in Jillian's career, so this was an added bonus. Upon my return, I immediately contacted our corporate attorneys to draft up a strategic-advisor agreement for Billy. In addition, Billy expressed an interest in investing in Yellow Brick Road and told me his business manager would be in touch with me.

As we worked on Billy's advisor agreement and engaged with his business manager, more good news streamed in. I received a call from the Software Association of New Hampshire informing me that Yellow Brick Road had been selected to receive the governor of New Hampshire's "Rookie of the Year Award." We were

> As you know, one of my parallel objectives in starting Yellow Brick Road was to further Jillian's chances for success in the music industry. I figured I would be meeting and helping a ton of people, and, over time, they might return the favor and help me with her career. At a minimum, I figured they might be more willing to listen to her latest demo or to offer her an opening slot at a big show. As things played out, however, Jillian decided to de-commit from the music business in favor of living a traditional teenager's life. After my experiences, I must say I am very pleased she made the choice to bow out of the scene for a while and to focus on going to school and enjoying her friends. Not surprisingly, six years later, Jillian was back in the business—writing, recording, and performing.

selected for the work that we were doing on BandDigs. Our corporate attorneys had nominated us for the award. Suffice it to say, the selection committee was really impressed with what we were building and with the high-growth prospects of BandDigs.

I was invited to a meeting with Governor John Lynch for the presentation and was asked to present at the Software Association's annual dinner. I'd be lying if I didn't say I felt pretty cool about this. It was further validation that we were onto a major opportunity. First, Virgin, then Aeropostale, then Billy Mann, and now the governor. Could all of this really be happening? I was starting to plot where I would put all the cash that was surely due to come in any day now.

A few weeks after receiving the award, on December 1st, we finally launched the BandDigs beta site with limited functionality. I decided to hold off until January to do any press releases. I figured we'd use the month of December to expose additional bugs that we hadn't caught during our final testing. I got an email from the president of Inept congratulating me for going live. In a way, the note really pissed me off. What was he congratulating me for? Being five months late? Or for deciding to leave out some of the most important features of the site in order to be able to launch it five months late? More importantly, what would happen next? Did this mean that he felt like the pressure was off him to finish the project once and for all?

Yeah, you guessed it. We had boatloads of problems with the launch, and we would have looked *extremely* foolish if we had announced the site to the world. BandDigs was down more than it was up in the month of December. When it was up, we had tons of issues using the video chat and the video broadcast tools. One morning, just before an important client meeting, I checked the site and found our home page completely trashed by a friggin' hacker. Inept had forgotten to shut down a back door, which the hacker had exploited.

Obviously, I was pulling my hair out at every turn. I tried to keep my cool with Inept, but it was extremely difficult. By this time, I had tried every project management trick known to mankind to try to manage Inept and the project schedule. They just didn't get it. They used every excuse in the book and basically said that all sites like BandDigs went through this, e.g., Myspace and Facebook.

My reputation was now seriously in question with my investors, and I was not pleased by this. I had announced the site launch to them, and they couldn't understand why the site was so unstable after being five months late. Since I had picked Inept for the project, I had to walk a fine line between throwing them under the bus and propping them up in the eyes of my investors.

As I mentioned earlier, I had nowhere else to go at this point. If we fired Inept, it would mean starting all over again, and we would potentially lose the code that they had developed up to that point. My only leverage was withholding payments to them on the basis that the development work was still not complete. If they wanted to get paid the final 33% of their contract, they needed to complete the development work to my satisfaction.

Here is the weird part, though. After two weeks of going live, virtually none of our pilot artists or pilot businesses had complained about the technical issues. Since we hadn't heard from them, I decided to call most of them personally to fall on my sword and explain what we were doing to stabilize the site.

As I would come to learn, none of them were actually using the site, so they hadn't even noticed the problems. This was an early sign of trouble ahead. If our pilot artists, who were given real incentives to work with the site, weren't using it, what would new bands do with the site (especially when we gave it to them for free)?

My holidays in 2006 were consumed by working with Inept to repair the site and then retesting it. We planned a press campaign in January, and I did not want to back off that. We desperately needed to generate some buzz for what we were doing if we were ever going to be able to attract the bigger funding required to commercialize the site.

After we convinced ourselves that the site was more stable, we issued the following press release nationally.

BandDigs.com Gives Bands Global Exposure, Fans Unprecedented Access

Online Community for the Music Industry Launched by Yellow Brick Road Entertainment

Windham, New Hampshire, January 7th 2007 - Yellow Brick Road Entertainment LLC announces the launch of www.BandDigs.com 1.0, a first-of-its-kind interactive music web community that revolutionizes the way bands and fans communicate. Bands utilize BandDigs to video chat with their fans (large numbers of people at once) and to stream live video broadcasts from back stage at venues, their rehearsal spaces, recording studios and even clubs. By joining BandDigs, subscribers increase their potential audience to millions of people around the world.

According to Yellow Brick Road Entertainment Founder & CEO Garry Wheeler, "Our goal was to provide bands with interactive technology once only afforded by large corporations that would enable them to take their careers to the next level. We wanted to take the concept of an online social community to a new level. Literally within minutes of subscribing to BandDigs, a band can be broadcasting live around the world like they own a TV station, or they can be interacting with their audience face-to-face."

Joe Fletcher (President of Joe Fletcher Presents www.joefletcherpresents.com and Fletcher Management) had this to offer about the site; "BandDigs levels the playing field for artists of all sizes and genres. It also allows music related businesses to reach customers in a new and meaningful way."

Keith Denehy from the well traveled and successful band Angry Hill www.angryhill.com , stated "BandDigs gives us the chance to talk live with our fans, share videos, broadcast all our live shows and the best thing is you can see us from anywhere and at anytime. I think this is gonna be killer and the fans are gonna love it!"

Musician-Tested, Fan-Friendly

For the last several months, Wheeler, a veteran chief information officer from the high-tech industry has guided BandDigs through an extensive test marketing process. This included granting full access to the site to nearly 50 recording artists and music businesses putting the site through its paces. The result is a web-based platform that offers the benefits of technology and community access to musicians. BandDigs already has artists on the site who are signed to labels such as Virgin Records, RCA, Motown, Columbia, Nonesuch, Vagrant, Fueled by Raman and Immortal.

Music businesses including record labels, management companies, gear manufacturers, venues, promoters, and producers currently use expensive web conferencing services for communicating and delivering training, consulting services and product demonstrations. BandDigs CEO, Garry Wheeler, explains, "BandDigs replaces these conferencing tools for about half the cost and also provides additional features such as the large interactive video chat space and live video broadcasts. These features can be cool options if a company wants to showcase its product or services or, better yet, interact face-to-face with their customers."

According to Wheeler the new technology has the potential to change how bands evolve and market themselves. "This creates an unequaled opportunity for bands to interact with fans from a one-on-one to a global basis and get immediate feedback as they create, test and change their material, image and branding in real time with the fans around the globe," Wheeler concluded.

Fans Gain Unprecedented Access

What makes BandDigs different for fans is that they actually get to talk to their favorite recording artists using their webcam face-to-face. They don't just receive "be my friend" requests and text updates. Fans get to provide the band real-time feedback about songs, shows, videos, CD artwork, etc. Fans can record all video chats and live video broadcasts and make them available for download on BandDigs so they can keep a copy for themselves on their computer, i-Pod and even on some cell phones.

Fans can easily participate in group chat rooms with their favorite performers and watch free live video broadcasts. They can also earn prizes by promoting bands to others. All they need to do is create a free account on BandDigs and then become a fan of the bands they like. Fans get their own pages on the site and their own video BLOG space designed to help them tell others about the bands that they support. Fans can also purchase premium services such as one-on-one recorded video chats with their favorite bands.

Ben Consoli, lead singer for the very popular Boston based band Violet Nine www.violetnine.com, offered "Our favorite thing about BandDigs is the video chats. All we need is a webcam and all our fan needs is a computer and we can talk."

About Yellow Brick Road Entertainment LLC:

The Software Association of New Hampshire and Governor John Lynch presented Yellow Brick Road Entertainment with the "2006 Rookie of the Year" award for the BandDigs.com product. The award is given to companies who demonstrate "cutting edge technology, a coolness factor and the potential for explosive growth."

Yellow Brick Road Entertainment is a privately funded New Hampshire based company dedicated to creating and applying technology solutions that revolutionize the relationship between recording artists and their fan base worldwide. For additional information or to arrange a site demo, Contact: Sales & Marketing 877-544-BAND, # # #

This announcement and subsequent follow up coverage on our launch generated a fair amount of interest and more importantly (website visits). We sent e-mails to every band that we knew with the following promotion:

ABOUT BANDDIGS – www.banddigs.com
A First of its kind online meet and greet music community!

BandDigs is a unique interactive music web community that is revolutionizing the way bands and fans communicate! Bands use our site to video chat with their fans and to stream live video from cool places like back stage at venues, their rehearsal spaces, recording studios and even clubs. By joining BandDigs, overnight you will have increased your audience potentially to millions of people around the world! Bands can even chat with their agent, manager, record label, the media and even with their family and friends back home when they are on the road!

What makes BandDigs different for fans is that they actually get to talk to their favorite recording artists using their webcam face to face. They don't just receive "be my friend requests" and text updates. Fans get to provide the band with regular feedback about songs, shows, videos, CD artwork, etc. Don't worry, even if you don't have a webcam right now you can still join in on the fun. If you have a microphone (most PCs have them built into the keyboard) you can participate in the chats with your photo showing on the screen and your voice being heard. You can also watch the video chats and the other live videos that the bands broadcast on their pages. On BandDigs, all video chats can be recorded and made available for download so you can keep a copy for yourself on your computer, i-Pod and/or some cell phones - pretty cool!

Fans can easily participate in group video chat rooms with their favorite performers for free and can even get a sneak peek behind the scenes (during rehearsals, in the studio, at clubs/venues & sometimes even on the tour bus). All you need to do is create a free account on BandDigs and then become a fan of the bands that you like. You get your own page on the site and your own video BLOG space designed to help you tell others about the bands that you support. The bands will then send you video e-mails and invite you to watch live streaming videos and to video chat with them on a scheduled basis. Fans can also purchase premium services such as one on one video chat time with artists and recordings of video chats with the band and streaming broadcast videos

Key Site Differentiators

- Music only subscription based community (bands & fans are free)
- Do it yourself live streaming video broadcasts (DV camera/webcam) to registered users
- Interactive video chats & polling with large numbers of fans or just one on one
- No special software needed to participate (PC and MAC compatible)
- Video BLOG/e-mail messaging (one touch recording)
- Artists approve advertisers and revenue sharing model/referral program
- Pay per view of events (optional) e.g. webinars/training, broadcasts, consulting, etc.
- Video recording and distribution capability (optional)
- Artists receive e-mail and demographic data of their fans
- Fan promotion incentive program, fan pages, video BLOGs (points/prizes)
- Integration with Myspace, YouTube, etc.
- Companies & professionals use the site for pay per view, web conferencing & training

In the three weeks following the press release, 150 bands and 400 fans had signed up. We seemed to be off to the races. New content was showing up on the site every day, including band and fan photos, songs, and videos. I figured the bigger pilot artists would be sending out invites to their Myspace friends, so it was just a matter of time before we had thousands of fans building their pages on BandDigs.

As mentioned previously, I pursued a number of strategic consulting partners, looking for ways to generate free promotion for BandDigs. I focused on companies that would not see any conflict between what they were doing and our platform. Initially, I just wanted their help marketing our site to their customer base.

In turn, we provided each company with a corporate account on BandDigs that gave them access to all our tools. We also equipped them with banner ads on BandDigs to increase their exposure to our subscriber base. Just as I'd hoped, these various partners began to tell their customer base about us, and we saw an additional 50 bands and 300 more fans sign up in February. Not a lot of traction, but something.

As the site began to gain momentum, Sully Erna, lead singer of the band Godsmack gave me a call. One of my friends in my town knew Sully and suggested he check out what I was doing. Sully suggested stopping by my office so I could give him a full demo of the site. We met, and, as usual, we had some technical challenges due to Inept. Luckily for me, I covered them up for the most part. Bottom line, Sully left our meeting seemingly totally pumped up about the site. He called his manager in Los Angeles and the president of his New York City record label and convinced them to meet with me in New Hampshire.

At Yellow Brick Road headquarters—a.k.a. the basement of my house—we hosted Sully, his manager Paul Geary, who worked for Irving Azoff, and Monty and Avery Lipman from Universal Republic Records.

The presentation really kicked ass (I had customized it for their artists), and the demo went very well for a change. We showed all the tools working, and the more we showed them, the more excited they seemed to get. It was all I could do to curb my enthusiasm at the meeting. My primary goal was to get Godsmack on our site. I also was hoping that Monty and Avery might be interested in investing in us and/or acquiring BandDigs at some point. Godsmack's fan base was gigantic and loyal. They would undoubtedly deliver thousands of fans and considerable buzz in the industry.

One of my better New York City contacts, Shep Goodman, had just accepted the role of vice president of A&R at Universal Republic, so I figured we'd surely be able to follow up and capitalize on this opportunity.

At the meeting, however, Sully had some reservations about using the site. He said, "After touring most of the year and finally getting home, I'm not sure I'd feel like taking time away from my family to go online and talk to fans." In general, he liked the concept for other bands (maybe bands that weren't as well known), but not for Godsmack's purposes.

About three quarters of the way through the meeting, I started thinking to myself, *Why would these music industry experts/executives come all the way to New Hampshire to learn about what we were doing?* Based on the questions that they asked and the overall tone of the meeting, my gut told me they were thinking of doing something similar on their own and they were just trying to learn how complicated it was to pull off. At the end of the meeting, Sully said he would be in touch and drove off with his team.

The following week, we hosted yet another demo/customer visit with Bose Corporation (the audio equipment guys). Bose was thinking of using BandDigs to train field techs and to host product demos for their customers. The meeting went extremely well, and it looked as though we were poised to land our first paying corporate account.

Investor 6 was good friends with Fred Bramante, founder/CEO of Daddy's Junky Music (retail chain of music stores in the Northeast). Fred was also interested in what we were doing and came by for a full demo. My hope with him was that we'd be able to add Daddy's as a corporate user and that we'd get them using the video broadcast tools for the music clinics they hosted in their retail stores. I was also hoping to attract Fred personally and/or Daddy's as investors in Yellow Brick Road.

We agreed to a plan to add Daddy's to BandDigs and to conduct live webcasts from several upcoming store events. Fred invited me to his quarterly sales managers meeting to present the concept and to demo the site. Many of the store managers talked to me after the meeting to let me know how excited they were about BandDigs. One of the more excited store managers was Hirsh Gardner of the 70's band, New England (hit single "Don't Ever Want to Lose Ya"). Hirsh had all kinds of ideas for the site and planned to put it to good use.

While I was busy chasing my own leads, Richard Ellis, my strategic marketing consultant and a long-term music industry veteran, pursued a myriad of different options to get more music businesses and artists on the site. He and I were both invited to serve on panels at a digital media millennials event in Los Angeles, so he set up several meetings for us with his contacts in LA.

One of the more encouraging meetings was with VP of Marketing Paul Orescan and director of Media Technology Aaron Foreman at Geffen/A&M records. Just to walk through the doors of Geffen's headquarters gave me goose bumps. Geffen had worked with some of my all-time favorite artists, including, John Lennon, Elton John, Don Henley, and Neil Young.

For Geffen, we did an abbreviated demo of the site, but they really got it. They told us they would add several artists to BandDigs and in particular, wanted to include the Bratz (a young all-girl band) as part of their upcoming movie promotion. They suggested that we work through the details over the next few weeks and they'd make it happen.

In addition to Geffen, Richard arranged a meeting with the VP of marketing & promotion at Walt Disney Records. This man was equally impressed and had a few artists he could see working well on the site, so we agreed to work through the details when I returned to New Hampshire.

Lastly, we met with Founder and President of Fanscape, Terry Dry, a very successful artist promotion and management firm. They managed the band, My Chemical Romance (Reprise Records), amongst others. On the surface that meeting went well too, but the president wanted his IT guy (who was out of the office) to look under the covers with us the following week.

All in all, I returned from my trip totally pumped up by the prospects of all the California discussions. As soon as I got back to my office, Richard opened the door to the CEO of Rounder Records in Boston (one of the largest and most successful indie labels in the country) and the CEO of Newbury Comics (a prominent CD retail chain). All these opportunities that Richard harvested further demonstrated the need for a full-time person like him on my team. He was clearly worth his weight in gold, and he was only working a couple of days a week for me.

The CEO at Rounder, John Virant, loved my pitch and the demo. John had just returned from working with Robert Plant and Alison Krauss on their debut duet album. He volunteered a few choice stories and handed me a copy of their unreleased record to listen to. Perks of the biz! He then invited me to come back to his office a second time to meet with his marketing staff. He immediately gave us a couple bands to add to the site and seemed to quickly connect the dots. He saw BandDigs as an opportunity to create and sell additional content, e.g. video chats having a higher profit than selling songs/CDs.

At Newbury Comics, it was a little different meeting. Mike Dreese, the CEO, had suggested that he had seen sites like BandDigs come and go over the years and wasn't too interested in the idea. He voiced concerns about getting permission to broadcast in-store events, saying the managers and labels always make it tough on them to get approval. *Hmmm, my first reality check on my concept.* Oh well, on to other opportunities…

When my daughter Jillian had performed on the 2005 Camplified tour, she'd toured with Nikki Flores, a teen artist signed to Epic Records. I got to know Nikki and her mother very well over that summer, so I reached out to them when BandDigs was about to launch. I figured I would offer Nikki some additional exposure by being one of our featured artists. Nikki's mom opened the door to Epic for me, and they seemed interested in including Nikki after I walked them through a demo.

Subsequently, my sales & marketing manager knew a local producer, Anthony Resta, who had worked with the likes of Elton John, Fiona Apple and Collective Soul. She first met him through the band Angry Hill that she had managed for years. We went down to his studio in Chelmsford,

Massachusetts, and gave him a full demo of the site's capabilities. He was totally blown away and agreed to add his studio to BandDigs and committed to arrange a meeting with Collective Soul in a few weeks. He felt they would be a great fit for the site, and the site for them.

We then got a promising call from the Firm, one of the largest artist management companies in the world. They had stumbled onto BandDigs in their research of the web and were really interested in what we had to offer. They asked us to work with a new band called Fiction Plane. The band's lead singer was Sting's son, Joe Sumner. Fiction Plane was going to be opening for the Police on their upcoming reunion tour. The Firm wanted BandDigs to go backstage on some of the tour stops and broadcast live behind-the-scenes footage. What a great opportunity for us! Working with the Firm would surely open a ton of doors for us with other mega artists.

A few weeks later, I decided to contact Brad Delp, the lead singer from the band Boston. More currently, Brad led the band Beatlejuice (an incredible Beatles tribute band that he had been performing with for ten years or so). Boston had sold over 50 million records since the 1970s. I first met Brad when Jillian sang for him in a restaurant before one of his shows back in 1999. We went to the Beatlejuice concert that same night, and he dedicated a song to his "new friend Jillian and her family." I got to know him over several years in different circles and stayed in touch with him as a result.

We built Beatlejuice a great presence on BandDigs and prepared to feature the band just before Brad was scheduled to kick off a reunion tour with Boston. My hope was that once Brad got a feel for what BandDigs could do for Beatlejuice, he would then introduce me to Boston's manager, and we'd be positioned to make a big splash in the music community by offering backstage footage and live interviews of the Boston tour. I thought this could be our big break, especially if the band would agree to interact with fans via the video chat space.

~~~

At this point, you must be asking yourself: *Why didn't BandDigs take off like a friggin' rocket? How could a company blow this with so many great leads?*

Yeah, well, here it comes. I will now recap what happened in the following months with each one of these promising opportunities.

Sully Erna, Godsmack and Universal Republic Records

- I waited about a month and never heard anything from Sully Erna. I called him a couple times on his cell phone and left him messages, asking for some feedback from the meetings, but I never heard a word from him. I also contacted his manager, Paul Geary, who never called me back or returned my emails. I found this disappointing and unprofessional. Even if one of them had called me back to tell me the site sucked, it would have been better than not hearing anything at all.

Billy Mann, Record Producer and Manager of Teddy Geiger

- Billy Mann had his business agent follow up with me about his advisor agreement and his pending investment in Yellow Brick Road. All good, right? Wrong. Billy's requirements were far greater than we were prepared to offer him. He wanted a good chunk of equity to be involved. After six weeks of back-and-forth communication, I informed Billy's agent that we could not meet his requirements. Unfortunately, this decision also meant no Teddy Geiger for the site.

Daddy's Junky Music, Fred Bramante, CEO

- I went on to the do the dance with Fred and Daddy's Junky Music for months regarding them investing in BandDigs, only to come up short in the end for reasons I still don't completely understand. We did several webcasts from their stores, but things never progressed further on the investment side. Unfortunately, Daddy's ended up closing its doors a few years later.

Bose Corporation

- My contact at Bose got transferred to a new role in the company, and I was unable to spark any interest with the person who replaced him in the corporate subscription on BandDigs. It died on the vine.

Geffen and A&M Records

- Geffen couldn't get out of their own way to make anything happen. Even though the top guy in the company said "Go," every person in the food chain inside the label found reasons for not moving forward. Their digital media director was brutally honest with me at one point in the process. He said, "Why should I give you my artists so that your company can become the next YouTube? What's in it for us?" He wanted Geffen to have a piece of the action—founder's shares. This was problematic for me to agree to. If other labels found out Geffen was a part owner, they potentially might prevent their artists from signing up for BandDigs.

Disney Records

- After several months, Disney couldn't figure out what to do with the two artists they thought would be a good fit on BandDigs, so they never bothered to add them to the site.

Fanscape and My Chemical Romance

- Fanscape's IT guy was very partial to the site Stickcam and couldn't understand the benefits of BandDigs. Stickcam was a cool alternative to BandDigs, but it was not a music-only community, and it was owned by a holding company rumored to be in the porno business. Frankly, until then, I had not heard of Stickcam. **LESSON LEARNED #28: Know *all* your competitors.** I should have known about Stickcam. This site was so much easier to work with compared to BandDigs. It literally took five minutes to learn the basics and to start working with their tools. Had I seen this site earlier, I would have made several changes to our site design. I also would have decided to roll out less functionality to keep things simpler for bands and fans.

Rounder Records, John Virant, CEO

- John Virant at Rounder wouldn't return any of my calls or emails after the second meeting. At one point in my discussions with him, I had mentioned we were looking for additional investors. My guess is this turned him off, but I don't know for sure.

Epic Records

- Epic Records couldn't get their act together for Nikki Flores. I kept being handed off to someone else in the company and just couldn't close with them. At one point, we created a hidden page for Nikki and sent a link to Epic for them to check out. We included a video that Nikki had posted on her Myspace page to show an example of what her BandDigs page would look like. All Epic could say was: *Did you guys pay to license the video?* I explained that it was a just a demo and that frankly I didn't care if Nikki ate a peanut butter sandwich on BandDigs, so long as she engaged with her fans. My experience overall with the bigger labels confirmed what I had read about them for years. They simply didn't know how to embrace the web to promote their artists.

Anthony Resta, Producer & Collective Soul

- Well, like so many other opportunities, we were unable to reconnect with Anthony Resta. He wouldn't return our voicemails or emails. I'm sure he's a busy guy, but I'm hard pressed to believe he was any busier than I was at the time. Again, it was unprofessional on his part. Why not just say "no thank you" and be done with us? Who knows? But the sad part was that we lost Collective Soul.

Newbury Comics, Mike Dreese CEO

- Mike Dreese at Newbury Comics had said "No" in the first meeting, but indicated it was okay to contact him once we had some traction. I never bothered to follow because as he had projected, we couldn't gain the traction that we needed.

The Firm and Sting's son

- We did some work with Fiction Plane and the Firm, but as luck would have it (or no luck, in our case), our contact at the Firm left the company, so we never really got the recognition that we'd hoped for in working with Fiction Plane. After he left, we were unsuccessful at getting to the right people at the Firm to take our relationship further.
- Brad Delp & the Band Boston
- By far, the most troubling of all these lost opportunities was Beatlejuice and Boston. I received a phone call that made all the rest of these disappointments seem trivial. On March 9, 2007, Brad, at age 55, had taken his own life just a week or two before going

on tour with Boston. I still get sick to my stomach whenever I think of this. He was not only an incredibly talented performer, he was an equally great person. What an untimely loss for so many people. The day after Brad died, the band Boston took their website down and replaced it with the following statement: "We've just lost the nicest guy in rock and roll."

Virgin Records, Don Rohr

- To add further salt to the wound, my primary contact at Virgin Records, Don Rohr, left the company as part of the company's merger with Capitol Records. I couldn't get anyone that mattered at Virgin to return my calls or emails after Don was out of the picture.

By now, you get the idea. We had some early signs of success, and we had solid reasons to believe we were really on to something. Many industry execs had validated our thinking, we had several hundred bands that signed up, and we had opened doors to some influential industry folks. In a nutshell, however, almost as fast as the opportunities presented themselves, they evaporated and we were left wondering what to do next.

Chapter 8

THE DETAILS ARE DEVILS AFTER ALL

Out of respect for the privacy of my investors, I will continue to only refer to them by numbers 1-6, but will share some of the dynamics of the group and how it affected our results.

Unless you plan to file all kinds of paperwork with the SEC to sell shares in your company publicly, you must only accept money from *accredited* investors. This is important to note. If you are planning to call on your Aunt Martha for money, talk to your attorney first. She may not qualify based on the method that you use to raise capital for your company.

At the back of the book is the form that Yellow Brick Road investors had to sign to declare they were accredited (Exhibit G). This will provide you with the definition to work with.

Securing funding and investors was the area where I was weakest when I started the business, but by the end of the venture, I had become quite knowledgeable regarding the positives and pitfalls.

I will address these issues from the perspective of what I would do differently if I were to fund a venture like BandDigs again.

LESSON LEARNED #29: When you are looking for investors, try to find ones who really understand your industry and customer base. As I touched on earlier, money is clearly important, but your investors should bring more to the party than cash. Looking back, I would have been much better off trying to find an angel group with some experience in the entertainment/music industry to invest in the first round of BandDigs. Not only would the right group have offered expertise and contacts, they could have challenged my business plan and helped me to avoid crucial mistakes along the way. They could have introduced me to many industry folks and led me to the Series A round through the right VCs and/or strategic investors.

Certainly, all my investors were successful in their own area of expertise as I described earlier. The fact that they could afford to plunk down $100,000 for a good idea is a testimony to their prior business successes. The problem was that we all got caught up in the *concept* of BandDigs. I had the passion for the idea and the sales skills to sell it, and my investors were all looking for something new and exciting to invest in.

In the end, though, none of us had the experience in the music industry to make it pay off. Each of them had their own reasons for jumping in, but my guess is, if you asked them today, they'd probably all say that they let their emotions get the best of them. The thought of being involved with a cool technology in the entertainment industry, while other sites like Myspace and YouTube were taking off, was just too intoxicating for them to turn down.

None of us had the skill set to fully appreciate what we were getting involved with. In hindsight, I should never have asked my investors to invest in Yellow Brick Road to begin with. What business did I have asking these guys to entrust their hard-earned money to me, when I had never done anything of any significance before in the music industry? Sure, I had run my own businesses before and knew quite a bit about the web, but those roles had been in the high-tech industry that I knew exceptionally well.

I was junior at best when it came to the music industry, and I knew even less about raising funding for a venture like BandDigs. I was making it up as I went along. It was certainly possible that I could have stumbled onto something big, but the odds were not in my favor, and the investors I picked did not increase the odds. My skills as a former CIO helped me put on a great game face in every discussion. I never let anyone see me sweat. In fact, I was the pillar of confidence . . . until we were just about out of cash.

LESSON LEARNED #30: Know your own personal limitations before asking others to invest in you/your plan. In my case, I should have avoided falling prey to my emotions. I should have built a plan that allowed me to hire industry experts to either run the company or work for me, to compensate for my shortcomings.

It is not easy to contain your enthusiasm when you are passionate about your idea. If it wasn't for my passion, I wouldn't have been able to sell the concept to potential investors and to stick with it to finish the project. The problem was that I was a better evangelist than I was a CEO who could deliver on the promises in the plan. That said, if your business plan has you focusing on an industry that you don't have a wealth of experience in, I'd recommend you have someone who knows you and your background well to help you do an objective skills assessment. You really need to be fair to your potential investors, and to yourself for that matter.

Like it or not, I had attracted six investors to Yellow Brick Road, and I needed to make it work the best that I could. I met with them regularly to discuss our progress, to get their feedback, and to ask them for their help. I believed wholeheartedly in what I was trying to do, and I worked like a slave to try to make it happen for all of us. Unfortunately, *I didn't know what I didn't know* about the music business. I didn't allow myself to doubt what I was doing, for fear that it would undermine my ability to sell the plan to new investors.

Our meetings were generally positive affairs, even when things weren't going that well with the development. All the guys were genuinely nice people who were trying to find the positive in my updates. As I mentioned earlier, one of my investors had brought four of the other guys to the table, which created a team within the team dynamic. The sixth investor was somewhat of an outsider, so if anyone disagreed with his point of view, it was pretty much automatically discounted.

There were other issues here that my inexperience exacerbated. For starters, I lost track of the fact that I had a lot more to lose than each of my investors. Every one of them were in the financial position to "afford" to lose their $100,000; it would not have an impact on their lifestyle. In my case, not only was I risking my investment, I was working for half the salary that I could have made elsewhere, I put my successful career on hold, and I risked failing for the first time

> Shortly after launching BandDigs, I had thought about expanding the site to include different celebrities to grow our subscriber base faster. I figured if fans wanted to video chat with their favorite bands, they would also want to video chat with their favorite actor, professional athlete, author, race car driver, golfer, etc. Out of this thinking was born the FanDigs.com concept. I reached out to one of my good friends, Rico Petrocelli, a former Red Sox player—and a great one, I might add—to see what he thought of the FanDigs concept. I met Rico for breakfast and discussed the concept with him at a high level. He loved the idea and came to my office a couple of weeks later to see a full demo. He loved it even more after seeing the demo. He thought we might be able to get some of the retired players from the '60s and '70s in particular to try it. Rico could broadcast his own show over the Internet, and then he could take calls like a radio talk show host with the bonus of video. Richard Ellis also helped me test the concept with a book publisher and a teen magazine editor that he knew, and they also expressed a lot of interest. We immediately added this idea to our plan, figuring that we could leverage a lot of the work already done on the BandDigs platform to get the FanDigs site to market quickly and for short money. Ahhh, the ideas just kept coming. Unfortunately, due to lack of capital, the idea never went any further than the plan, some domain names, and a logo.

in business. **LESSON LEARNED #31: Remember, it is not all about your investors. You need to be cognizant of what you have to lose and protect it.** If I had recognized this earlier, I would have insisted on bringing in a music-industry-savvy executive to work for me, or for me to work for.

I could have stepped down to be the chief technology officer and let someone who really understood the industry take over the reins, make deals, and attract additional funding. If I had brought in the right CEO, he/she probably would have been able to secure additional funding for us through contacts that I never had. My experience with Richard Ellis had further justified the need for senior-level industry skills and meaningful connections. Be that as it may, I never even considered this idea.

Instead, I continued in the CEO role and did my best to lead the company as I know how. In that capacity, I was invited to present at the MIT Enterprise Forum sponsored by the New Hampshire High-Tech Council. I figured the exposure would be worth the preparation time.

Rather than do a PowerPoint presentation like the other presenters planned on doing, I ran our BandDigs promo video to start off the night. It ran about five minutes long on the huge screen over the PA system and blew people out of their seats. We received a lot of great feedback, and I made a few new contacts who looked like they would lead me to new angel investors or investment bankers. I left the meeting feeling very proud of what we were building and of myself.

LESSON LEARNED #32: Don't let your ego own you. I got so caught up in accepting awards, making successful presentations, and meeting bands and label execs that I lost my perspective. I took my eye off the prize. The prize would have been a multimillion-dollar round of investment to commercialize BandDigs, not the short-term satisfaction of running a business in an industry that I aspired to work in. I got totally caught up in "playing doctor."

When we began to really struggle to raise the next round of funding, I made the statement to my investors that I was trying to protect them from losing their investment. This statement was immediately met with pushback from the group. They were concerned I wasn't thinking BIG enough. They expected me to focus on making them a lot of money, not protecting them from losing it.

Moreover, they reminded me that when we had decided to not charge for subscriptions, it was with the goal in mind to go for the big kill. They decided to forgo short-term revenue in favor of driving up the registered-user base to create higher multiples. The goal was to think big all the time, and I was thinking small by trying to protect them from losing their money. Again, this was a sign of my inexperience talking.

LESSON LEARNED #33: Play the role of entrepreneur and embrace the risk all the way to the end. I should not have allowed myself to act like a small-business owner who managed the downside. By definition, a play like Yellow Brick Road is a high-risk proposition. If you can't play the game or afford to take the risk personally, then you have no business being the CEO of a startup. My investors were prepared to lose their investment, but I was not. I believe this hurt us in the end.

Question for you, reader: Can you live with having a bonfire with the cash you are planning to invest in your own venture? Would you be able to toast marshmallows as the fire burned? If not, DO NOT try this at home. Keep your day job.

For you first-time entrepreneurs, allow me to shift gears and tell you where I focused my efforts over the course of the two-plus years that I ran

Yellow Brick Road. For the most part, I worked six to seven days a week. During a normal week, I would work from 7AM to 9PM and Saturdays from 8AM to 7PM and Sundays from 8AM to 1PM.

Working out of my house meant I didn't have a commute and I got to see my family passing through on most days, so it seemed like I was at least staying in touch with them. I had to travel to Boston a couple of times a week to meet with Inept, to visit potential investors, to see customers, to go to shows, and to meet with alliance partners. I also drove down to New York City many times and traveled out to Los Angeles to meet with the labels and management companies.

During the first year, as you would expect, I spent the majority of my time in the following few areas:

1. Writing the plan
2. Lining up funding
3. Defining/developing the site

After the first year, I spent my time

1. Begging for more funding
2. Developing the site
3. Re-writing the plan
4. Promoting the site.

Part of promoting the site included going to shows at different venues, seeing bands who were in town from other parts of the country, and meeting with lots of managers. There were many late nights for these types of meetings and events. The sales & marketing manager would go to a lot of shows to either webcast the show live or to get video of the shows to put on BandDigs. Some of the clubs really liked the concept, and it gave us a chance to show off the technology in a live environment to bands and fans.

At this point, we were in late spring of 2007. Again, I have highlighted the task dates of items started or completed by then. (Green = on time, Yellow or X = 1-6 months late, Red or XX = over 6 months late).

Task	Planned Start	Actual Start	Planned End	Actual End
Create business plan	Nov-05	Nov-05	Apr-06	Apr-06
Build prototype	Jan-06	Jan-06	Feb-06 X	Mar-06 X
Seed funding presentations	Dec-05	Dec-05	Apr-06	Apr-06
BandDigs site development	Jan-06	Jan-06	Jun-06 XX	Partial XX
50+ person chat space dev	Jan-06	Jan-06	Jun-06 XX	Partial XX
Seed round funding	Apr-06	Apr-06	May-06	May-06
Pilot artist events	Apr-06 X	Aug-06 X	May-06 X	Oct-06 X
Beta site launch	Jul-06 X	Dec-06 X	Sep-06 X	Dec-06 X
Site launch and press release	Sep-06 X	Jan-07 X	Sep-06 X	Jan-07* X
Series A funding presentations	Sep-06	Sep-06	May-07	
Series A funding	Jun-07		Jun-07	
Investment bankers engaged	Not planned			
Presentations to acquirers	Not planned			

After five-plus months of going live, we had 300 bands and businesses registered on the site that had over two million Myspace friends. Thirty of the 300 bands were signed to labels such as Virgin, Columbia, RCA, Geffen, Disney, Bad Boy, Rounder, Vagrant, Universal, and Nonesuch. We had many other deals in process with businesses, labels, management firms, venues, and radio stations. In May, we had three million hits on the site so the traffic looked promising.

All good, but we had a few red flags flying in our faces. First, with 300 bands registered, I was expecting quite a few fans to register on the site. If each band just brought 50 fans with them, we would have had 15,000 fans registered by this point. Well, we only had 1,500 (10% of what we were expecting). An average of five fans per band! Hardly even a drop in the bucket.

To put this in perspective, nine of the bands had over 500,000 Myspace friends, and yet, on BandDigs, they only had a total of 400 fans who had signed up for an account! The more troubling red flag was the lack of video chats or live broadcasts that were showing up on the main calendar of the site. If each band ran one event per month, we would have ten events on the calendar every day of the month. Instead, the only events showing up on the calendar were the ones we were running at venues and with our pilot artists ourselves.

Of the 300 bands registered, only about half of them had invested the time to build their basic page on the site. Some had registered several months earlier and still hadn't created their page, despite our frequent reminders. Yeah, this was a little bit troubling, but looking back, very indicative of the music business. Remember, bands just want to focus on their music.

Lastly, we offered free training two nights a week to bands on the site to explain how to use the video chat and video broadcast tool. Not a single band attended, despite us promoting the training to all registered bands on a frequent basis.

This takes us back to **LESSON LEARNED #24: Really know your customers.** I lost track of this on more than one occasion. We made a fundamental mistake in our design. We underestimated the need for simplicity above everything else. If a band had to spend more than ten minutes learning how to use our site, they simply weren't going to do it.

I had to ask myself why the pilot artists hadn't said something to us earlier, but then again, I already knew the answer. Except for a few bands, none of our pilot artists had used the site or the tools on their own. They had their interns work with the site, or they relied on our interns to help them. None of the band members had invested the time to learn the tools, so why would they have provided us with feedback on ease of use?

Each of our pilot artists did record welcome videos for their pages that we also used to promote the site. Almost all of them were videotaped and uploaded by me or by members of my team. Only two or three bands created their own videos and sent them to us to upload.

When we ran events with the pilot bands for the site, we did all the heavy lifting. I only know of a couple of our pilot artists who tried to use the tools on their own, and they were more tech savvy than most bands were.

One of these groups was B5 from Georgia. They were signed to Bad Boy Records (P. Diddy's label). They had the desire to regularly use the tools with their fan base. When B5 told their fans about BandDigs, hundreds of new fans registered on the site in a few days. Jillian had actually been on the same concert bill as B5 a few months earlier and I had met them and their Manager at the show.

B5 had some crazed fans, just the type of fans that we wanted on BandDigs. Their fans not only signed up, they spent the time to build elaborate pages for themselves and to promote the group across the site. They emailed customer service, asking when B5 was going to be doing their next video chat so that they could attend. They were passionate kids! It was really exciting to see this type of interest from both the artist and their fans. It reaffirmed that fans were really interested in the BandDigs concept (at least for the right band).

B5's manager, Jim McMahon, called me to let me know about a couple of events they were planning to have on the site. He wanted to make sure that BandDigs could handle the web traffic before they promoted the events to their audience. They'd apparently run into some issues while using text chatting on AOL the month before.

According to Inept, we had a robust infrastructure, and it could handle anything a band could throw at us volume wise (unless, of course, it was someone huge, like U2). One of our volume controls was the registration system. Fans had to be registered on BandDigs to participate in B5's planned events. This gave us a pretty solid indication of the potential site traffic for a live event. I told Jim to bring it on. The band scheduled a couple of test events to try out the tools, including a rehearsal session that allowed the fans to interact with the band members backstage via video chat. B5 had some challenges with the tools during the rehearsal, but we attributed it to a bad Internet connection. The band had used a wireless card in a remote area that had marginal service.

A couple hundred or so viewers had watched their event, which began with showing the band in their motorhome. The fans were so frantic that some of them videotaped their computer screen and then posted the video of the event on YouTube. The band basically just took questions and then responded to them live, using the video broadcast tool.

A month later, B5 had planned a live concert broadcast with a video chat after the show. We promoted it to the fan base on our site and issued a press release to support the event. On the night of the show, BandDigs suffered a complete meltdown. No one at Inept could be reached to help solve whatever was wrong, despite us giving them a heads-up before the event. Hundreds of fans had registered to watch the event, and they couldn't even log in, let alone watch it. That was the end of B5 on our site. They never bothered to come back, and neither did most of their fans.

We were up to about 3,000 fans on the site at the time of the event, of which almost half could be attributed to B5. So, not only did we lose a hip band from Georgia, we lost half our user base thanks to one site meltdown. I will say this, the fans kept coming back looking for B5. But once they figured out the band wasn't coming back, they left in droves. Of course, when I finally got in touch with Inept, they had their regular laundry list of excuses prepared. They just didn't get it! They repeated their go to defense that Myspace had early problems too. As I reminded them, Myspace did not meltdown with just 3,000 users on their site as we had.

LESSON LEARNED #34: If a large number of your customers will be trying out your product at one time, make sure it works—or at least have a backup plan in case something goes wrong.

We should have insisted on having Inept do formal stress testing on the site beforehand to predict our breaking point. We should have also had Inept's team available during the event to attend to the technical issues in real time. Instead, we went down in flames that day.

In the 2 charts below, you can clearly see the impact that B5 had on the site statistics by month when they first joined and then when they quit using the site.

Stats by Month from Launch to the end of 2007

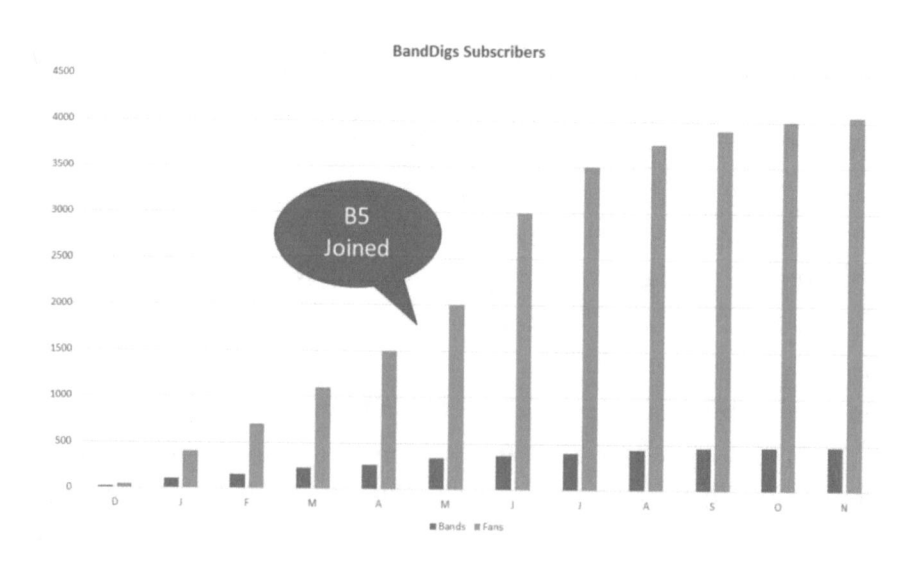

BandDigs Subscribers

(B5 Joined)

UNIQUE BANDDIGS HITS

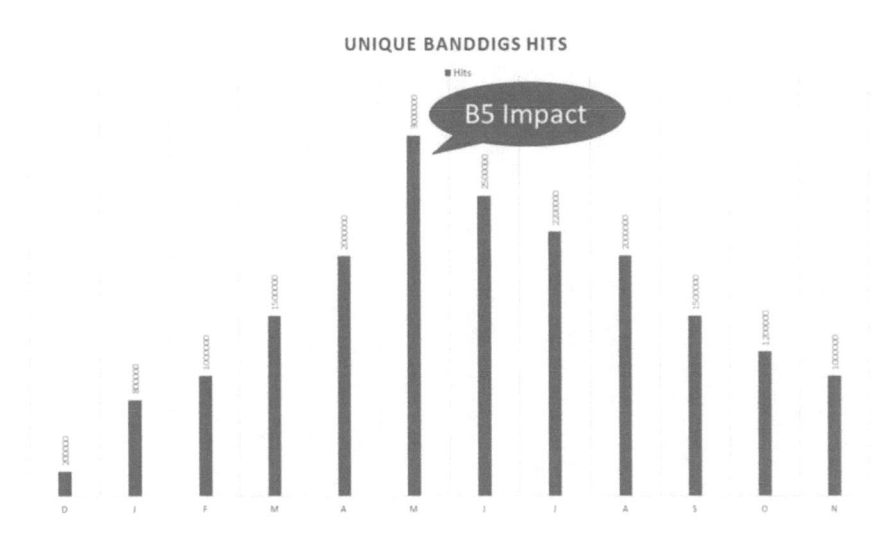

B5 Impact

Another interesting dynamic worth noting was our registration process for fans. In hindsight, we clearly expected fans to tell us way too much about themselves when they registered for their free account. I am sure this scared off a bunch of users. It was an intimidating form, and much of the information was just not that important for getting people to sign up. **LESSON LEARNED #35: Make it easy for your customers to engage with you**. Ask for the bare minimum info from your new customers. Once they become a regular customer, you can follow up with them to ask for more.

Chapter 9

HOW DO YOU DEFINE TRACTION?

From December 2006 to November 2007, I spent more than half my time trying to raise additional funding

I attended VC and angel investor events, presented at various investor forums, pitched VCs and angels in person, on the phone, via their web submission tools, and in plain old email. I networked with banks, lawyers, and investors who weren't in our industry, with alliance partners, with the record labels, managers, producers, with VCs who had told me "no" already, and with my own business contacts. I called the local press to get coverage on the company with the hope of surfacing new individual investors. All this was done with one purpose in mind: to raise at least $2 million in additional capital to support our commercialization effort. I needed to find my fix!

The 50+ person chat space was finally delivered in August of 2007—a full year late by Inept. It didn't have all the bells and whistles, but it was in good enough shape to demonstrate to potential investors. The main problem was that it recorded the video chats in two separate streams (video and audio). Inept still hadn't worked out merging the streams into one file so that a fan could download it to their iPod or computer. Remember, the point was for fans to be able to show their friends that they had spoken to their favorite band, and we would charge them for the download.

NEW 50+ CHAT SPACE SCREENSHOTS

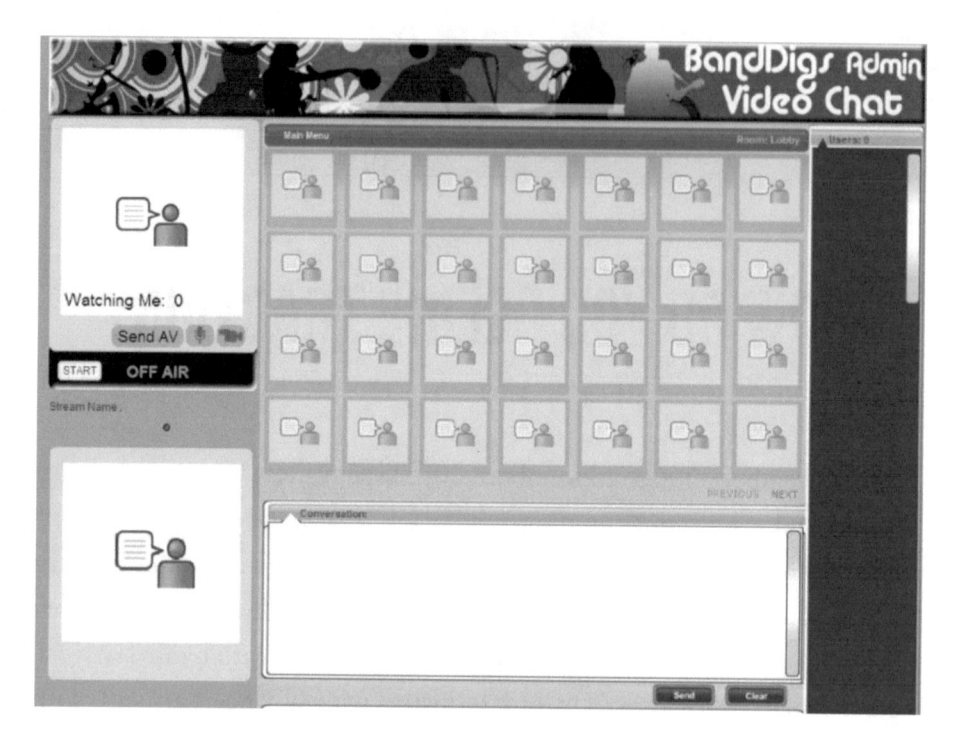

RECORDED STREAMS

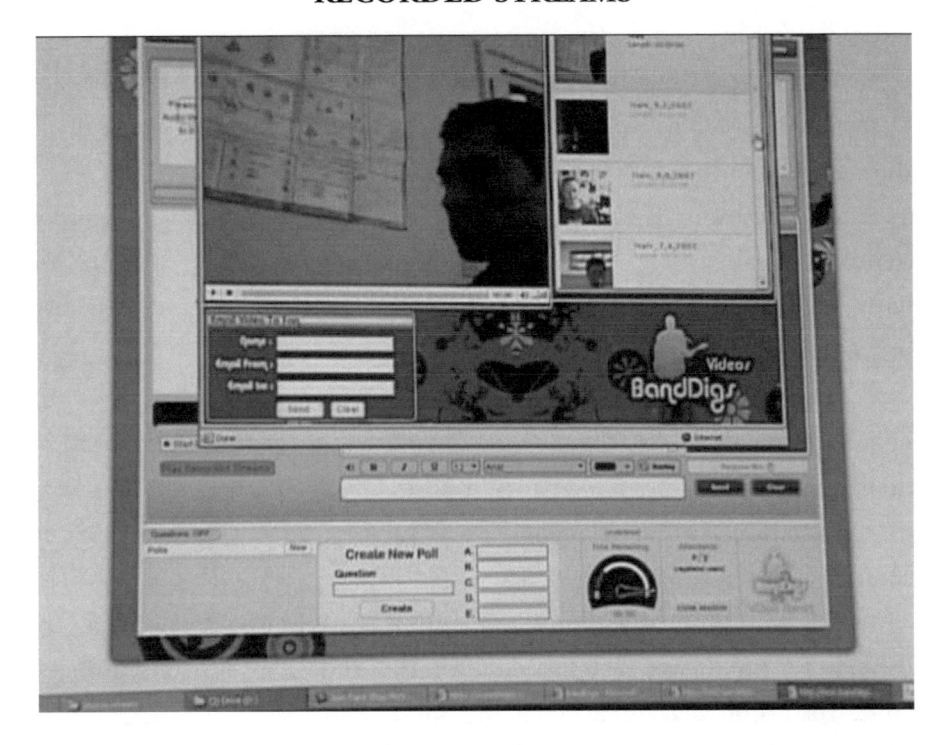

Throughout the funding process, I heard many investors, especially VC firms, speak of *traction*. "Come back to see us once you have some traction to show us." "Good idea, but we don't see enough traction yet to jump in." "Great concept, but we need to see the traction." **LESSON LEARNED #36: If you're not sure what a potential investor is saying, ask!** When you present your plan to a few people and you keep hearing something that you really don't understand, stop and ask them what the hell they're talking about. In my case, I thought I understood what they were looking for, but I really didn't. I assumed that they meant "show us that the bands and fans are using the site as you intended them to." What they were really saying was "We're concerned the market size for BandDigs is limited and it will be tough to monetize the site."

As I came to learn after talking/meeting with roughly eighty firms over the course of eighteen months, most VCs look for companies who have a chance of growing to over $1 billion in sales. With so many people illegally downloading music, they weren't convinced we could sell enough content or advertising on the site to grow anywhere near that. They needed to separate BandDigs from all the other "noise" in the industry to confirm their interest in it.

That said one firm that expressed interest in our plan was Venrock Ventures. I really thought they were going to jump in after my first meeting with them. One of the potential angel investors that I had met with had introduced me to Venrock.

Conversely, after my second meeting with them and a short site demo, Venrock said "no thank you." Then they proceeded to ask me to be their lead presenter at the Web Innovators Group meeting the following month (go figure). If nothing else, it told me that we were still working on something interesting.

The Web Innovators Group presentation was one of the highlights of the year for me. It was further validation that BandDigs was cool and creative. The event was held at the Royal Sonesta Hotel in Cambridge, Mass. There must have been close to five hundred people (investors, tech-savvy folks, and fellow entrepreneurs) in attendance.

We started the demo by showing a live show at a Boston club and then switched over to a video chat backstage with the band's manager. All this was projected on a huge screen similar to a live TV show and was tied into a fantastic PA system. It was an impressive demo, and we received many accolades for it in blogs all over the Boston area.

BLOGS DISCUSSING OUR PITCH

BLOG 1 – www.93.south.net

The surprise of the night was Windham, NH based BandDigs which creates online video channels and interactive applications for bands. The service is a very cool capability for up-and-coming artists but my concern before the show with BandDigs was that it appears to be just another band listing site.

However, Garry Wheeler's demonstration of their live streaming video and 50-person video chat application makes me wonder if there is a larger business concept that will develop from this local start-up? There is already a buzz right now around live video streaming sites like Justin.tv and Mogulus so half of their offering is timely but that chat application was very cool…I may even use it for an upcoming conference call.

BLOG 2 – www.ucredible.com

Now, without further ado, here are my post-event impressions.

Main Courses

BandDigs - is a video/video chat site for bands and fans. I checked out a few band pages, watched some videos, etc. The site made me think Stickam meets Myspace - not a bad thing; and I can certainly see the appeal if you are a) a band wanting to create a stronger connection with your fans or b) a fan that wants a closer connection with your fave band. At the end of last year I met with a company (whose name I probably shouldn't mention) with a technology that promised a similar experience. The biggest difference was that theirs was a desktop application. BandDigs seems like a much better approach. One thing that impressed me was the number of live events already taking place.

I had a chance to chat with BandDigs President Garry Wheeler before things got underway and he confirmed many of my impressions of the company. There were a couple of things that I hadn't realized. One was that bands are using this for more than just presenting live music or scheduled chats. Some are taking fans backstage or onto the tour bus. It's also being used to survey fans and do Q&A sessions. On the business front, Garry described an interesting option. Fans are able to record a video of themselves talking with band members which they can purchase through the site as a keepsake. Kind of cool I guess if there's a band you absolutely love.

Expectation that I'll be wowed - given that I'm not a real hardcore fan of any bands, I don't expect BandDigs to be something that's going to have me rushing home for video chats any time soon; but I can certainly see the appeal in what they are doing and am expecting to at least be impressed. Hopefully *they'll be able to do a live demo that will include connecting with one of their bands on the 9th.*

They did include a band in their demo but I couldn't tell if it was live or not (I don't think it was) as well as a live chat with a band manager. The live chat was pretty cool. It supports 50+ people and allows private video chat between fans (critical for killing time as you wait your turn to speak with the band one-on-one). A couple people felt that BandDigs was a bit rough around the edges but that didn't strike me as a major issue.

Chances that I'm way off base - pretty low. These guys have a good idea, a solid site and strong content.

I'm pleased to say that I was on target with BandDigs. I like what I saw and can see the appeal of the site to bands and fans alike.

Unfortunately, even though this coverage was compelling, the red flag was that we did not receive any new inquiries or interest in our funding request. Investors still questioned the business model.

LESSON LEARNED #37: Know the profile of the investors you are pursuing. Most VCs focus on specific industries or geographies when they invest, and they look for synergies between a company already in their portfolio and the new ones they are considering. Other VCs focus on the stages that companies are in, e.g. seed, early term ($0 revenue) versus later term (revenue and customer base). The VCs in the Boston area were not that familiar with the music industry to begin with. I wasted a lot of time chasing VCs who had no intention of funding us. We either didn't fit their industry or their stage of investing.

Andrew Metrick in his very insightful 2007 book, *Venture Capital and the Finance of Innovation*, offers the following about VC firms:

VC firms are small organizations, averaging about ten professionals, who serve as the general partner (GP) for VC funds. A VC fund is a limited partnership with a finite lifetime (usually ten years plus optional extensions for a few years). The limited partners (LPs) of VC funds are mostly institutional investors, such as pension funds, university endowments and large corporations.

Most VC firms specialize their funds by stage, industry, and/or geography. For example, an early-stage fund would make initial investments in early-stage companies, with some capital reserved to make follow-on investments in these companies in their later stages. A late-stage fund would typically avoid all early-stage companies, focusing on expansion and later-stage investments. Most VC firms keep the same stage focus for all their funds, but some will change focus over time or mix the two strategies at once in a multistage fund. A few firms raise separate early-stage and late-stage funds for overlapping periods and assign different professionals to each fund.

There is a wide dispersion in the levels of industry focus, with many generalists (a fund that is willing to invest in both IT and health care is effectively a generalist) and others with a relatively narrow focus on sectors like energy or financial services. As for geographic focus, it is important to recognize that much of the activity experienced by VCs is local, and as a result the location of the VC's office will usually be highly correlated with the location of most of their portfolio companies.

Angel Groups pretty much follow the same path as VCs, plus they look for companies that their individual investors can help with. In other words, they're not going to invest in a biotech play unless they have investors in their own group who have a biotech background. Typically, angel groups want to take an active role in the companies they invest in.

Man, I wish I had read Andrew's book before I started Yellow Brick Road! I would have known I was barking up the wrong tree with some of the VCs I was chasing.

At the back of the book is the executive summary I used with angel and VC investors (Exhibit H).

I'd like to say that the more I presented the plan, the better I got at it. The reality is that it got monotonous making the same pitch over and over again. Hearing "no" or "come back when you can show us traction" gets really old. It really felt like I was tin-cupping on a street corner or trying to sell vacuum cleaners door to door, day in and day out.

My most discouraging meeting occurred in June of 2007. As I mentioned earlier, with Angel groups, you generally meet with a sub-group first to qualify your plan, and yourself for that matter. They typically don't want to waste the whole group's time reviewing ideas that don't fit their profile.

In May, I had submitted my business plan online to a very prominent investment group, The New York Angels. The founder of Jamspot (the Boston-area rehearsal space for bands that we had used to test BandDigs) had referred me to the group, so I was able to list his name on the online submission form. To be honest, I didn't think I would hear back from them, but to my surprise, they invited me to present my plan to their review committee. They first screened me on the phone to make sure I wasn't a complete loon (little did they know).

They gave me a format to follow, which I found very helpful, but it took me a couple of days to organize my standard pitch to comply with it. I hit the road at 4AM and fought the traffic to arrive in New York City for my 10:30AM time slot. While, sitting in the lobby on the thirty-fifth floor for at least an hour, I couldn't help but notice my fellow entrepreneurs parading in and out with their laptops and presentation materials. Most of them looked a lot younger and seemed extremely confident in the way that they carried themselves.

I must admit that I was taken back a bit by the amount of activity and started wondering if I was wasting my time. The odds did not appear to be in my favor, at least. Anyway, I was finally invited into an overcrowded board room. There must have been twenty-five people crammed in a room that comfortably sat fifteen, and I could barely get to the front of the room to set up my laptop. The room was very stuffy, and it reeked of burnt coffee and stale pastries. I made a lighthearted comment about the journey down from New Hampshire that morning, and it went over as well as a fart in church. The group was not interested in any small talk and emphasized that I had no more than thirty minutes to make my presentation. Ouch.

It was hard for me to fathom the egos in that room, and to make matters worse, I was sure they were all Yankee fans (just kidding - sort of).

As I started my pitch, I realized this was a very different group than the ones I was used to presenting to in the Boston area. They challenged every slide and every assumption. It was brutal. I started to sweat five minutes into the meeting. Fortunately, the blood had drained from face by that point. My skin was so pale that the sweat just blended in on my forehead. As miserable and embarrassing as this meeting was, I couldn't help but wish it had happened a year earlier in my process.

One of the biggest revenue sources in the BandDigs plan was advertising on pages and in front of/during live events. Yet, when they drilled me on my assumptions about site visits, impressions, etc., and asked me to defend my calculations and my click-through rates, I realized I didn't have a clue about this portion of the plan.

They went on to test me on the details of the marketing plan, which I wasn't prepared to speak to in any detail either. Lastly, they wanted more information about our licensing model and our assumptions about the content on the site—all of which I also struggled to answer.

Bottom line, I left the meeting with my sweaty, pale head in my hands. I then faced a six-hour drive home in heavy traffic so I had plenty of time to reflect on the meeting. It was one of the worst experiences I've had in my career. As I was sitting in traffic in Hartford, Connecticut, I got a call on my cell phone from the guy who invited me down to the meeting. He wanted to let me know that they were going to have to pass. I didn't even bother to ask for feedback. I knew I had totally blown it.

He did go on further to advise me that I wasn't going to be invited to present to the larger group. Big shocker! Frankly, part of me was relieved. I couldn't imagine what it would have been like dealing with an even larger group of those experts (and egomaniacs). **LESSON LEARNED #38: Make sure you know every financial detail included in your business plan—and reduce it to memory!** If you don't have the expertise to complete the details yourself, hire someone who does and make sure they explain everything in detail to you. In my case, I should have hired a marketing consultant to help me with the online advertising assumptions, click-through calculations, and related details, so that I could have defended the plan accordingly. Not only would I have avoided this humbling ordeal, I might have gained some new investors.

After the New York Angels experience, I did spend a fair amount of time documenting the online advertising assumptions and producing the data to back up my calculations. I then continued my quest to secure funding. In preparation, I created several versions of the funding requests, including a bridge-round version that called for just $500,000 while we searched for bigger funding. Over a twelve-month period, I contacted close to one hundred potential investors in some form or fashion to no avail.

> Readers, it would be interesting to hear from you to learn about any experiences that you have gone through analogous to my New York Angels presentation. On the website for this book: www.ybrentertainment.net, there is a page where I share some of my readers' "New York Angels" moments in their careers. Please use the contact form on the home page to submit your experiences, so we can all commiserate in one place and learn additional lessons from each other. You can also email me at garry@garrywheeler.com.

I previously mentioned the quality of the format that the New York Angels had me follow. See below for the outline of the format that I used at the meeting. In the appendix (Exhibit I), I have included the full presentation that I gave by following it. The format was well received everywhere, and it fit with angel groups across the board.

1. Vision statement
2. One page product overview – Don't get into the bits and bytes… keep it to a functionality level and describe the business issues that your product is intended to solve

3. Our team/brief BIOs
4. Market sizing data & drivers
5. Pain points – What does your product/service help to solve?
6. Top level business strategies
7. Sources of revenue
8. Sizing of customers/market
9. Primary competitors
10. Barriers to entry
11. Financial summary
12. Funding request detail

It wasn't long after the New York Angels meeting that I had to approach my current investors and tell them we would be out of cash in a few months if we couldn't find new sources of funding. In July of 2007, I asked them all to consider putting more money in to help carry the company long enough for me to raise the capital. I told them I would cut my salary in half until we landed the next round of funding if they would agree to put in $20,000 each. Back to **LESSON LEARNED #12: Pay yourself what you are worth.** Don't offer to work for a reduced salary. I was already drawing from my home equity line to pay my bills, and yet I offered to cut my salary. From June until December, I worked for $1,000 a week, a mere quarter of what I was making in the corporate world.

Just after putting this offer on the table to my investors, I got a interesting call from the very well-connected Editor of *Paste Magazine*, Jay Sweet. *Paste* was a high-end music "tastemaker" magazine that included a music sampler CD each month. It was one of my favorite magazines, so it was cool just to talk to Jay. He was referred to me by one of my local music contacts and offered to meet me for lunch to understand how he might be able to help us. I felt like Jay might be my savior, so I jumped on his invitation.

Jay loved the whole BandDigs concept. We spent a lot of time talking about how the site fit with Myspace and YouTube. At the end of the discussion, Jay offered to connect me with some investment bankers in Boston that he felt could really help Yellow Brick Road.

Consequently, Jay introduced me to Nick MacShane of Progress Partners in Boston. I started out doing a walkthrough of the plan and a site demo over the phone with Nick and his team. Progress expressed a lot of interest in Web 2.0/Cloud and even in the music industry and told me they had other clients directly in our sweet spot. Nick asked me to come to his Boston office to discuss the next steps.

At this point, I really felt that I needed to include my investors directly in the meeting vs. me going in alone. My hope was that they would get excited about the idea and be more willing to put some more money into the company to hold us over while Progress helped us. Investors 1 and 2 wanted to attend the meeting with me while the others agreed to meet with us after for a de-briefing.

Both guys attended the first meeting with me. We had lunch together after the meeting and basically talked through the pros and cons, and at that point, there were many more pros than cons. We met with the other investors as planned and they also agreed.

Progress Partners easily convinced us that we needed them to help us raise capital. We all really believed this was THE answer for us and were ready to put our fate into their hands. Toward that end, they offered us a contract that started with a formal business assessment, business model/plan feedback, etc., which we would need to pay for upfront.

Following the assessment, Progress would have the right to disengage if they didn't feel they could help us raise funding. We, of course, would have the option of accepting their proposal to engage. If we accepted their proposal, we would need to pay them a monthly retainer, and then a percentage of the funding raised.

Seemed like a "no brainer" to me, but we had one "minor" detail to overcome. We were running out of cash! Even with my reduced salary, we were spending close to $20,000 a month for salaries, computer leases, software maintenance, support, etc. Back to my investors . . .

I brought up the need for cash again at our late August meeting and presented the Progress contract offer to them. I reached an agreement in principle with five of the six investors (the sub-group led by Investor 1) to each invest another $20,000 in two installments. $10,000 now and $10,000 after Progress completed its business assessment and agreed to take us on as a funding client. Investor 6 declined to invest any further.

Prior to engaging formally with Progress for money-raising purposes, I spoke to four CEO references whom they had provided me. Once I was satisfied that they could do what they said they could, we got started on the assessment process. This process was educational and enlightening. Investor 2 participated in the process with me this time. Investor 1 was out of town. Investor 2 shared his experiences with the other investors, which helped to legitimize our decision to engage with them. Again, we were blown away by the work that Progress did for us in such a short period of time.

I *really* wish I had met these guys a year earlier. They studied our industry, our plan, our technology, our competition, and then identified potential strategic partners and funding sources. They challenged me and the business model. At the end of the process, they convinced us that we should be licensing our platform to the record labels, management firms, radio stations, etc. instead of pursuing a strategy like Myspace (giving the site away to build up a large user base).

This was a very interesting angle, and one I had considered when some of the labels expressed concerns about BandDigs seeing all the web traffic instead of their artist or label sites. The beauty of such a model would be the immediate dose of revenue that would come from it. The downside was the upfront investment required to be able to accommodate such a model technically.

See the following paragraphs for the critical gaps and recommendations that Progress reported to us. This action plan would serve as our revised game plan. We shared this with new prospective investors and rebuilt our financials around this approach.

Capability

- Reorganize service offerings to customers including packaging the white label services and renovating BandDigs website to best meet user's demands.
- Identify and hire key business development person(s).
- Initiate partnership discussions with content and ad distribution companies.
- Addition of content manager and technology operations team members.
- Better understand financial models and economics of operation.

Business Development

- Develop advertiser pipeline.
- Develop white label client pipeline to hedge against slow user uptake in BandDigs community.
- Develop mid-size label and management company pipeline.
- Addition of sales vp from the music industry with label/management company network.

Assessment of Market Dynamics

- Concentrate on local market initially to develop user base.
- Concentrate on assessing market receptiveness to interactive video services in music industry.

Long term Strategy

- Online music service industry is highly fragmented and crowded with a number of existing players, with a few powerful social networking companies controlling more than half of the market.
- BandDigs should explore options for expanding into other industry verticals outside of the music industry as a provider of white label technologies.

Probable Funding Strategy

- A venture round is not recommended before BandDigs figures out a potential horizontal expansion opportunity and develops key pipelines.
- We suggest BandDigs raises $0.5MM from existing investors or angels by the end of 2007. A couple of $MM will be required in the subsequent years, but accessibility to venture capitals will be low due to the limited size of addressable markets. It is highly likely that existing investors will have to continue to support BandDigs for expansion.
- We recommend establishing a 10% option pool for hiring key executives.

In effect, to support such an approach, we would need to create a "widget" that would work on other sites. Basically, the video chat or the video broadcast tool would need to show up on a band's website directly, instead of on the BandDigs site. BandDigs would provide the computer and networking infrastructure behind the scenes to run the tools from the different websites.

Since our tools were never designed to act as "widgets" on other sites such as Myspace or Facebook, we would need to make some coding changes and figure out how to support the backend infrastructure requirements.

Inept sized the effort to be around $80,000 worth of development work that required eight to ten-weeks to complete. By this time, I obviously knew I could not trust these estimates.

Progress felt if we were able to make the shift and land some customers, then they could raise us the additional funding required to make a go of the business. They also told us that, even if we pursued such a strategy, we would NOT be candidates for VC funding. They explained that the market (traction) was just not big enough to attract VCs. We would need to focus on angel investors and/or strategic investors to fund the company. I couldn't help but think about how much time I had wasted chasing VCs for two years!

Progress's team presented their findings and recommendations to me and my investors and convinced us to engage them to raise the required funding. Once we found these guys, it made it even easier for me to justify taking a pay cut while we landed the bigger fish. I just knew the big money was right around the corner, and then I could pay myself back many times over. **LESSON LEARNED #39: Don't get overly excited about anything until the money is in the bank!** It is still a business and not a round of golf. My emotions got the best of me here and clouded my judgment.

We now needed to finalize the contract with Progress . . . and here is where things fell apart. The contract was onerous, and none of us were happy with it. I asked our attorney to provide some feedback, and I let him know not to nitpick, since we were close to being out of cash and we really needed to make the deal work. Well, the process still bogged down considerably. While we tried to negotiate the contract, we were burning cash and Progress wasn't helping us. My investors felt like they were trying to take advantage of us by using stall tactics to negotiate the contract, knowing our cash was dwindling.

My investors became increasingly uncomfortable with the whole process and, in the eleventh hour, decided not to move forward with Progress. They also decided not to invest the second installment of $10K each. They had lost faith in Progress and decided not to throw their good money after bad. At that point, I'm sure they had lost faith in me as well, but they were too kind to tell me. This placed an immediate strain on Yellow Brick Road. We were unable to make our hosting and support payments to Inept in October.

For months prior, I had kept the president of Inept informed about our financial status, but he still acted really surprised when I called to let him know we were unable to make our monthly payment. I scraped together enough cash to pay for the first two weeks of October, but had to tell him we could not pay any more unless a miracle happened.

Subsequently, I contacted Progress to let them know we had decided not to engage them on a retainer basis. I told them if they brought us a buyer or interested investors, we would be happy to pay them their normal commission/fees for any transactions that they helped to facilitate. They agreed to shop BandDigs around to their contacts and to let us know if they stimulated any interest. I figured they probably had been testing the market while they worked on our assessment. I was hoping they may have had a few investors already in their back pocket that they planned to approach formally once we executed the contract with them.

This, of course, was the beginning of the end for BandDigs. As it turned out, Inept had signed a contract for BandDigs' hardware and hosting that they were unable to break, even though we stopped paying the fees. Consequently, they told us that they would leave the website up for demonstration purposes until they could either find another customer to take over the hardware that BandDigs was using, or until their contracts/leases expired with their vendors. It was obviously in Inept's best interest to keep the site up as long as possible so that we could demonstrate it to prospective investors or buyers. It was their only hope of getting paid, so they weren't doing us any real favors.

My investors were aware that unless something happened in the next couple of months, the site and the company would be shut down. They also knew I was going to spend most of my time searching for a full-time job. They did think, however, that even after the site shut down, I might be able to find a buyer for the platform. Unfortunately, I knew I would not have the time to do much once I landed a job. Moreover, I knew the money we owed Inept would be a big detractor to any potential buyer, so I did not hold out much hope beyond whatever Progress might be able to do for us.

In the end, Progress was unable to surface any investors during the six months of working with us. Deep down, I do wonder how much they would have been able to help us even if we *had* contracted with them.

Although Progress didn't identify any investors, within a few weeks, they did surface two potential buyers for the company and/or the BandDigs platform. In my mind, anything would have been better than nothing, so I was open to talk to anyone. In fact, I was contacting everyone I knew in parallel, offering to sell our platform to them.

This all came too late in the game for us, as our backs were against the wall with Inept. We owed them about $13K for some development work plus $35K in license fees for the new chat space, although this was never agreed to contractually and the chat space development was never completed. We also owed them for a half month of hosting support and hardware lease payments. Bottom line, Inept would be looking to be paid by someone.

Frankly, I was ready to be done with Inept and the whole damn project. I would have been thrilled with selling the platform for just about any figure in late 2007.

Here is where we were on the timeline. All the tasks except for the 50+ person chat space with recording capability and the Series A round of funding were completed by this time, albeit the development was more than a year late. (Green = on time, Yellow or X = 1-6 months late, Red or XX = over 6 months late).

Task	Planned Start	Actual Start	Planned End	Actual End
Create business plan	Nov-05	Nov-05	Apr-06	Apr-06
Build prototype	Jan-06	Jan-06	Feb-06 X	Mar-06 X

Seed funding presentations	Dec-05	Dec-05	Apr-06	Apr-06
BandDigs site development	Jan-06	Jan-06	Jun-06 XX	Jun-7 XX
50+ person chat space dev	Jan-06	Jan-06	Jun-06 XX	Partial XX
Seed round funding	Apr-06	Apr-06	May-06	May-06
Pilot artist events	Apr-06 X	Aug-06 X	May-06 X	Oct-06 X
Beta site launch	Jul-06 X	Dec-06 X	Sep-06 X	Dec-06 X
Site launch and press release	Sep-06 X	Jan-07 X	Sep-06 X	Jan-07 X
Series A funding presentations	Sep-06	Sep-06	May-07 X	Dec-07 X
Series A funding	Jun-07 XX	NA XX	Jun-07 XX	NA XX
Investment bankers engaged	Not planned	Aug-07	Dec-07	NA
Presentations to acquirers	Not planned	Sep-07	Jan-08	Jan-08

*The site was launched in Jan-07 with only partial functionality.

SLIDES USED TO EXPLAIN YELLOW BRICK ROAD BEING FOR SALE

Why Are We Looking to be Acquired?

- Our strategic consultants (Progress Partners) analyzed the industry and re-directed us to private label our main tools under a fee based business to business model vs. our current free business to consumer approach on BandDigs.com
- We've built some cool technology, started to see some traction for it, but are undercapitalized to support the commercialization of what we have to support the implementation of the revised business plan
- We lack the capital required to take the product to the next level (enhancements, API for licensing, marketing, etc.)
- We are looking for a company with deeper pockets and additional industry contacts to acquire the technology/platform and/or community and run with it
- New skills & contacts will be required to sell/support private labeling options

October 2007   (603)-898-0800 - Yellow Brick Road Ent. Patent Pending Technology

YBR Assets Available for Sale

- BandDigs Community & Features (15 months of development & testing)
- 50+ webcam V-Chat with Recording & Other Interactive Features
- Interactive Flash Broadcast Tool with, 1 on1 Chat & V-Blog

| Traction (400 bands/company subscribers & 2500 fans) |
| Private Labeling Option for the tools & customer leads |
| Infrastructure Designed and Built out |
| Patent Pending Status, Trademarks & Copyrights |
| Business Plans & Analysis Work |

October 2007   (603)-898-0800 - Yellow Brick Road Ent. Patent Pending Technology

In addition to our outstanding debt to Inept, which a buyer would need to repay, we faced having the site shut down at any moment when Inept found another customer for the hardware that BandDigs was using. Lastly, we had no staff left, as I had to let everyone go earlier in the month. Moreover, I was looking for full-time employment elsewhere. Trying to salvage some type of quick deal, our pitch to the potential buyers put all of this on the table up front, which immediately devalued the business. Essentially, we just wanted to sell the platform, not the business.

LESSON LEARNED #40: Don't borrow trouble for yourself. We really didn't need to mention the financial trouble or talk about me leaving until we got down to the financial negotiations. We should have tried to keep these potential buyers on the hook longer by avoiding these "touchy" subjects too early in the presentation. My job should have been to create a compelling reason for them to own our platform, irrespective of anything else that might have been going on.

Instead, we scared off the two potential buyers that Progress had identified for us. In one case, the buyer was just interested in licensing our tools, and in the other case, the buyer needed me to stay on full-time to run the business, but they weren't willing to pay me enough to make the deal work.

After the second potential buyer said, "no thank you," we realized we were out of options and out of time. The site remained online, but Progress informed me in late January of 2008 that they were no longer interested in spending time shopping BandDigs to their contacts. My last-ditch effort was to list the site for sale on a variety of business-for-sale websites.

Nothing came of this last-ditch effort, and on March 1, 2008, Inept Solutions pulled the plug on BandDigs; it became vaporware once again. We never even communicated our shutdown to the user base, as Inept had pulled the plug without warning.

LESSON LEARNED #41: You may be better off working for someone else. Looking back on this entire experience, I may have been better off staying in my corporate job and never attempting to do something so far out of my element in my late forties. The grass is not always greener, as it turns out. That said I did learn more in those 2+ years than I would have learned working for anyone else. If you do decide to jump in, just make sure you capitalize on the experiences of other entrepreneurs like you are doing by reading this book to be better prepared.

Here is a very critical **LESSON LEARNED #42: Be cognizant of the 1244 stock-loss rule and invest accordingly.** I almost made a serious error by not taking advantage of the 1244 stock provision. I assumed that I would only be entitled to the $3,000 maximum capital loss each year on my personal taxes. Instead, I found out through our corporate accountant that I was eligible to write off my total losses in the same year that YBR was shut down. In the appendix, you will find the details of this stock-loss provision (Exhibit J). If your venture should happen to fail, you will want to take full advantage of this. To take advantage of this rule, you must have invested directly into the company to obtain your shares of stock, which is what I had done.

This law entitles you to take the full loss of your investment in one year. Unless you invest the money into the company, you cannot claim the loss. This could have been a major lost opportunity for me. Knowing about this provision saved me more than $30,000 in federal taxes personally the year YBR was shut down.

Chapter 10

THE AFTERMATH: LICKING MY WOUNDS & GETTING BACK ON THE HORSE

In September of 2007 when I cut back on my hours at Yellow Brick Road, I had started to do some part time consulting work at a local project management training company, mScholar Corp. The CEO brought me in for two-and-a-half days a week to help her flesh out her business model and to develop a plan that would help her to expand the business.

The company offered a course that prepared project and program managers to take the PMP (Project Management Professional) exam, certified by PMI (Project Management Institute).

To better prepare myself for an impending full-time job search, I studied for the PMP exam myself for several months and then passed the test and earned my PMP designation in December. I also joined the board of directors for the Software Association of New Hampshire and acted as a judge for the annual InfoXchange awards. I did all this while I continued to work pretty much full-time at Yellow Brick Road, trying to fund/sell the business. I figured that I needed to get back into the swing of things to better prepare myself for the job market.

Three weeks before Christmas of 2007, I accepted a full-time job offer at Polycom Corporation as director of the program management office for their Telepresence Division (life-size video-conferencing). I knew the senior VP of services there from my days at Digital Equipment Corporation and had done some networking with him in October when things looked very grim for Yellow Brick Road. The telepresence technology really blew me away and Polycom was betting big on growing the division.

Instead of being excited about my new opportunity, however, I woke up the day after I agreed to take the job and felt like a complete failure. I had never felt so defeated before. The reality was starting to set in. I had just accepted a job at the same salary I was making when I worked at Polaroid eleven years earlier. I just couldn't afford to spend six months or longer looking for a better paying job. I had to stop the financial bleeding that I had suffered for over two years, so I was appreciative of the offer. I also took a few steps backwards from an executive VP/GM to a director level position.

Basically, I started over in a new company at almost fifty years old. Ouch! It was a very humbling experience trying to reestablish myself and to bring my A game to a job that I had done many years before. This whole experience took its toll on my confidence and slowed me down a step or two in the process. I had to work harder than ever to try and reestablish myself, but I really didn't feel as effective as I once had been.

Putting the job aside for a minute, I must say that avoiding a full onset of depression took every ounce of my being. For more than six months, I carried around a sense of guilt, failure, remorse, shame, and a financial burden. For eighteen years, my wife had not needed to work for us to pay our bills. She had been able to stay at home and take care of our kids. YBR and I put her in the position where she needed to go back to work full-time once my oldest daughter left for college to help me right the ship financially.

Due to my liberal use of the home-equity loan, our mortgage payment almost doubled. We ended up selling the beautiful house that I had built eighteen years prior and we moved to a townhouse to regroup financially. By borrowing on the house, in what turned out to be a declining real-estate market, we really took a hit on the equity. My original goal was to retire early, but that looked like an impossible task post BandDigs.

As you can imagine, I was not the happiest, most upbeat guy to be around following the shutdown. Daily, I had to face my wife and kids, knowing how I'd let them all down while finding enough energy to re-start my high-tech career in a very competitive environment. In addition, I had to face some of my investors/friends who lived in my town, realizing that I'd cost them $100,000+ and had disappointed them greatly. My friends all asked me what had happened, and I droned on regularly about the missed opportunity and biggest failure of my career.

Not even two months into my new job, I suffered a serious attack of atrial fibrillation that landed me in the hospital for a few days. I then had to give up some of my life's pleasures, namely caffeine and alcohol, while the doctors tried to figure out what had caused the attack. I also fought off being tired every day from the prescribed beta-blockers and tried to convince myself I was still a capable provider. I am totally convinced the stress caused by my failure at Yellow Brick Road brought on these health issues.

Just five weeks after the attack, I turned fifty years old. I had planned to go away to my favorite resort on the coast of Maine for my birthday with my family and some of my friends. However, I just couldn't find the energy or the reason to go, so we canceled the trip. The point is: failure takes a LOT out of a person. **LESSON LEARNED #43: Do not become an entrepreneur if you can't deal with failure.** The odds are stacked against you.

According to the Bureau of Labor Statistics' Business Employment Dynamics, here's what the survival rate looks like:

- About **80% (four-fifths)** of businesses with employees will **survive their first year** in business. (The most recent data shows that of the small businesses that opened in March of 2015, 79.9% made it to March of 2016.)
- About **66% (two-thirds)** of businesses with employees will **survive their second year** in business. (The recent data shows that of the small businesses that opened in March of 2014, 69.4% made it to March of 2016.)
- About **50% (one-half)** of businesses with employees will **survive their fifth year** in business. (Data shows that of the small businesses that opened in March of 2011, 51% made it to March of 2016.)
- About **30% (one-third)** of businesses will **survive their 10th year** in business. (The most recent data shows that of the small businesses that opened in March of 2006, 32.8% made it to March of 2016.)

What you really need to know is that about 20% of small businesses fail in their first year, and 50% of small businesses fail in their fifth year.

I should have spent a lot more time exploring my tolerance for failure and for financial loss before jumping in. Prior to Yellow Brick Road, in thirty-plus years of working, I had never really failed at anything. I was always in control of my own destiny, and I never took on such a high-stakes financial risk. Having established set criteria for my decision-making upfront would have helped me to manage the downside. I should have developed target dates for funding, and if I missed them, I should have had a backup plan, e.g. working part-time as a consultant earlier on, getting my investors or additional investors to put more in to pay my salary, or shutting down sooner.

LESSON LEARNED #44: Make sure your spouse or significant other agrees with your use of personal funds to launch the business and to keep it alive. I had a general agreement with my wife, so I was not sneaking behind around her back. That said she wasn't involved in the day-to-day decisions about using our home-equity line. Had I talked to her each time I was writing a check, I'm sure I would have been pressured to deal with the issues sooner and would not have let the emotions get the best of me. She could have been more objective—or not, for that matter—and could have challenged me to really think before spending more money on BandDigs. I had obviously convinced myself, like I had with my investors, and believed my own bullshit.

As you might expect, the torture continued for me each and every day for months, and that is the main reason why I decided to share my lessons with you. I am hoping they will help you avoid similar misery. I also hope you will contact me via www.ybrentertainment.net or at garry@garrywheeler.com and share your own experiences or your thoughts on my journey.

The only consolation in all this was the fact that I never touched my kids' college funds and that I found a decent job when I absolutely needed it. Also, fortunately, my health problems were not that serious. I had to pick up the pieces and try to show my kids that I could battle back from adversity. This would have been a lot easier to do if I had tried this in my thirties versus late forties. With the sale of the house, my wife working and my Polycom salary, our financial situation did improve substantially.

LESSON LEARNED #45: Make sure that you are fully prepared for the type of sacrifices you will need to make in order to run your business. As soon as you bring investors into your venture, you automatically have more bosses than you've ever had before. If you are driven like I am, you will be talking to them at all hours of the day and night. You simply can't escape the work. It completely takes over your life, and you justify the absorption because it is *your company*. You tell your family that no one else will do it for you. You wish you could join them for dinner or for a long weekend at the beach, but you just can't afford the time. All for what… money, freedom, being your own boss, living your dream job? The odds are not in your favor to begin with. Please leverage my 50 impactful lessons to be better prepared!

LESSON LEARNED #46: Hobbies and interests rarely make good business ventures. In my case, my judgment was clouded and my objectivity was compromised due to the emotional connection I had with music, bands, and my daughter's career. This really impaired my ability to focus on the business issues and on the increased debt I was accumulating each month.

In short, these were just a few more of those dreaded mistakes that eventually caused me to say, "Goodbye, Yellow Brick Road Entertainment." On that note… **LESSON LEARNED #47: Don't take money from friends and family unless you are prepared to lose them in your life.** This was a really tough lesson for me. I feel I have lost at least two important friendships. Don't get me wrong; the two investors who were my friends before BandDigs don't appear to hold anything against me. It is not them—it's me who has a problem with it. I have had a very difficult time going back to the way things used to be.

About a year after I shut down Yellow Brick Road, I went to counseling for depression. It really helped me sort out some of the "lessons learned" in greater detail. It also allowed me to work through the guilt I was feeling and helped me manage through the stress the business had caused me. I also began a regular exercise program, which helped me both mentally and physically.

LESSON LEARNED #48: It is more than okay to seek professional help. We do it all the time for things like accounting/tax prep, legal advice, annual physicals; so why not seek a professional counselor when you are not feeling mentally healthy? It really helped me to talk to an unbiased person and allowed me to sort through my first-ever feelings of "failure."

LESSON LEARNED #49: Make time for your significant other even while you are managing your startup. My startup only lasted two-and-a-half years, but my marriage has lasted thirty-five. Your family needs you even more than your business does. Don't take them for granted.

As far as my career post YBR is concerned, I stayed with Polycom for five years. I started out as a Director, but I was quickly promoted to Vice President. I ran operations & IT for the $250 million services organization for the first few years and then became the VP/GM for Polycom's global cloud services business (approximately $100 million in sales and 120 people). The last two years that I spent there, I received the company's top performance rating.

When the CEO of Polycom left to run a startup (Icontrol Networks) in the home security/smart-home space, he reached out to me 18 months later and I followed him as his senior VP of Operations. During my years at Polycom and Icontrol, I leveraged many of the lessons learned from my Yellow Brick Road experiences. They helped me become a better employee, leader, and manager. Many of the lessons have shaped me into the person that I am today in and out of the work arena.

In early 2017, after four years of very hard work at Icontrol, we sold the company to Comcast and Alarm.com, and my payday finally came. I was able to retire just before turning fifty-nine, and my wife at fifty-four. We then sold our house, cars, furniture, etc. and traveled the world together full-time to seventy three countries for almost three years before moving to Naples, Florida. Pretty much a fairytale ending after suffering the biggest failure of my career nine years earlier! We have since jointly authored a book about our full-time travel titled, *"Living Like You Mean It! - The Ultimate Guide to a Nomadic Lifestyle"*. It will be available on Amazon in the summer of 2024.

Through our travels, my wife and I have rediscovered each other. Our relationship is the best that it has been in thirty-five years. In addition to all of the travel that we have done together (over 100 countries in total), we now play pickleball and golf and go to live theater and art events together frequently.

In addition, I have enjoyed my hobby of racing stock cars (Richard Petty Experience, Dale Jarrett Racing and Rusty Wallace Racing) on the different NASCAR race tracks around the country. My wife gave me the first racing experience as a gift thirteen years ago. I have since raced on twenty-three different NASCAR tracks as of this writing. It is a thrill of a lifetime racing cars at over 160 MPH on these tracks.

LESSON LEARNED #50: There is life after a failed start up. Lick your wounds, and then get back at it with whatever experiences you've taken away from your startup and apply them to your next role. Your role as an entrepreneur can be leveraged in many ways, even if your startup doesn't make it.

Over the years, I have readily shared my experiences with others at work and with my friends. In fact, just recently I met with a couple of friends to help them sort through funding options for their wine-making business. Amazingly, most all my "lessons learned" transferred seamlessly to their venture. I found myself advising them to really think through the risks involved, to be crystal clear on their objectives, e.g. do you really want to make enough money to do this full-time? I asked them; "Do you want to work for yourselves or for a bunch of investors? Can you really work together as partners? Can you afford to lose your investment? What do your families think of the idea?"

It was through these conversations that I decided to finally share my story on a broader scale by publishing this book. Hopefully, you will be able to take these lessons and apply them to the business of your choice, and then ride off into the sunset—wildly successful! If not, at least you'll know someone else to reach out to when you are out there on the ledge.

Writing this book has also served as good therapy for me. It stimulated me to reflect on my entire career, and it made me realize I had a pretty good run overall. I had the experience of working with some great people and businesses; I'd made enough money that my wife was able to stay home with our kids for almost eighteen years, we could live in a beautiful home and we could afford to send our kids to great schools. I traveled all over the world and even landed on my feet despite saying, "Goodbye, Yellow Brick Road."

Continually, I have been able to leverage the 50 lessons as I pursue other areas of interest. For example, during the COVID pandemic, I reconnected with abstract painting and by the fall of 2020, I had launched my own art business and online store to market and promote my artwork. I have since gone on to win many international art awards and have sold well over 100 paintings in the U.S and Europe. My work has been in over 50 exhibits in Florida, California, New York, Italy and the UK and has been featured in various global art magazines and books. You can check out my artwork and read my artist bio at www.gswheeler.com

These same lessons also helped me as I transitioned to leading non-profit arts organizations in Southwest Florida. I am currently serving as the Board President of Marco Island Center for the Arts and the Art Center Theater. Before my current role, I served as the President of the Art Council of Southwest Florida.

The moral of the story is that it really is all about the journey and not about hitting it big with your startup. It's about learning lessons and applying them in your future endeavors. You might even hit it big elsewhere by doing so. My Dad, a very wise man, once told me that it often takes multiple failures in business to experience one true success. I guess I proved him right…. The only thing is, that I may not be completely done leveraging these lessons. As of this writing, I have been offered a role as COO and co-founder in an AI startup at the ripe old age of 66. Go figure! Keep a watchful eye out for my sequel.

Rock on!

~~~

I would greatly appreciate your candid review of this book. Please visit Amazon.com and share what you thought of the book with others. If you would like to reach out to me directly, you can do so at garry@garrywheeler.com.

50 IMPACTFUL LESSONS LEARNED RECAP

Lesson #1
Don't use your own money unless you can afford to flush it down the toilet.
This can save you your savings and your personal relationships.

Lesson #2
Don't assume your current business funding contacts will be able to help you in a different industry.
This can save you your life savings and your career.

Lesson #3
Develop and test your business plan with objective experts before quitting your day job.
This can save you your life savings, your relationships, and your career.

Lesson #4
When you are going to entrust your entire financial future to an outside vendor, do your homework, no matter who recommends them to you.
This can save you your savings, months of work, and your sanity.

Lesson #5
Validate your copyrights.
This can save you $25,000 or more.

Lesson #6

If you outsource a project to a vendor who takes twice as long than said vendor had promised to finish a prototype, re-consider giving them the contract for the full development effort.

This can save you $100,000 or more and many months of work.

Lesson #7

Know the rules when you are playing the game with venture capitalists (VCs).

This can save your company.

Lesson #8

Never start with your BEST funding option. Save them for later, once you've made a few mistakes and have tightened up your pitch.

This can save your company.

Lesson #9

Not hearing "yes" from a VC means "no thank you."

This can save you a year or more of effort.

Lesson #10

Do not write your business plan in a vacuum and DON'T believe your own BS.

This can save you your savings and your sanity.

Lesson #11

When you are creating and organizing your business plan, take time to write a couple different versions.

This can save you six months or more.

Lesson #12
Pay yourself what you are worth.
This can save you $100,000 or more.

Lesson #13
Find reasonably priced office space near your home that also gives you an identity with your customers and partners.
This can improve your personal life and give your business a serious boost.

Lesson #14
Take the money from investors when you can get it; cash is king. You will spend money faster than your optimistic plan calls for.
This can save your company.

Lesson #15
Bring in investors who can and/or who are interested in doing more for the company than just providing cash.
This can save your company.

Lesson #16
When you get a schedule from your outside developer, demand to see the details, including resource loading/hours, etc.
This can save you a year or more in product-development time.

Lesson #17
Include a bonus clause in the contract with your vendors for work done on time or a penalty clause for work delivered late.
This can save you a year or more in product-development time.

Lesson #18
DO NOT settle for someone who you can "afford" for a critical role.
This can save your company.

Lesson #19
If you want people to help you, be prepared to give them a share of the company or proper compensation in return.
This can save your company.

Lesson #20
Do not count on alliances to do your marketing and/or to bring you any new customers.
This can save you months in your effort to develop market traction and revenue.

Lesson #21
Clearly understand your IP ownership position and ensure that it is well documented between your company and your vendors.
This can save your company and can position you to sell your technology if the business goes belly-up.

Lesson #22
Don't take pushback from potential investors and/or acquirers too personally.
This can save you your sanity.

Lesson #23
REALLY know your customers.
This can save you your business and your cash.

Lesson #24
Get your product to market as quickly as possible, and test it with your customers as you move forward.
This can save you months in your effort to develop market traction and revenue.

Lesson #25
Don't surround yourself with passive investors.
This can save you your business and your savings.

Lesson #26
When you make a major change to your business model, take the time to contemplate the potential consequences.
This can save your business and your personal cash.

Lesson #27
Don't get caught up in the hype of other companies' successes—or failures, for that matter.
This can save you your sanity.

Lesson #28
Know ALL your competitors.
This can save your business and your personal cash.

Lesson #29
When you are looking for investors, try to find ones who really understand your industry and customer base.
This can save your business.

Lesson #30
Know your own personal limitations before asking others to invest in you and your plan.
This can save you your business, your life savings, your personal relationships, and your dignity.

Lesson #31

Remember, it is not all about your investors. Be cognizant of what YOU have to lose, and protect it.

This can save you your personal cash and preserve your most important relationships.

Lesson #32

Don't let your ego own you.

This can save you your dignity.

Lesson #33

Play the role of entrepreneur, and embrace the risk all the way to the end.

This can save your business and help you to attract new investors.

Lesson #34

When a large number of your customers will be demoing your product at one time, make sure it works—or at least have a backup plan in case something goes wrong.

This can save you months of work trying to build traction in the market.

Lesson #35

Make it easy for your customers to engage with you.

This can save you months of work trying to build traction in the market.

Lesson #36

If you're not sure what a potential investor is saying, ASK!

This can save you months of work in raising funds.

Lesson #37

Know the profile of the investors you are targeting.

This can save you months of work in raising funds.

Lesson #38
Make sure you know every financial detail included in your business plan—and reduce it to memory!
This can save you months of work in raising funds.

Lesson #39
Don't get overly excited about anything until the money is in the bank!
This can save you your sanity.

Lesson #40
Don't borrow trouble for yourself.
This can save you your sanity.

Lesson #41
Question if you would be better off working for someone else.
This can save you your personal cash, your career, your sanity, and your most important relationships.

Lesson #42
Be cognizant of the 1244 stock-loss rule and invest accordingly.
This can save you thousands of dollars in personal taxes should your business shut down.

Lesson #43
Do not become an entrepreneur if you can't deal with failure.
This can save you your personal cash, your career, your sanity, and your most important relationships.

Lesson #44
Make sure your spouse or significant other agrees with your use of personal funds to launch the business and keep it alive.
This can save your relationship.

Lesson #45

Make sure that you are fully prepared for the type of sacrifices you will need to make in order to run your business.

This can save your significant other relationship and keep your personal life intact.

Lesson #46

Realize that Hobbies and interests rarely make good business ventures.

This can save you your life savings.

Lesson #47

Don't take money from friends and family unless you can afford to lose them in your life.

This can save you lifelong relationships.

Lesson #48

It is more than okay to seek professional help.

This can save you your sanity.

Lesson #49

Make time for your significant other even while you are managing your startup.

This can save your relationship.

Lesson #50

There is life after a failed startup. *Hopefully you will exploit the other lessons and never need this one!*

ABOUT THE AUTHOR

Garry Wheeler is an award-winning and accomplished executive with forty years of experience as an entrepreneur, CEO, COO, general manager, program manager, and management consultant across multiple sectors, including high-tech, consumer products, manufacturing, real estate, professional services, and media/entertainment. He has an extensive background in P&L and operations management and has led many successful mergers and acquisitions.

His broad experiences range from startups to companies as large as $14 billion in sales. Since 1985, he has founded and operated five different businesses in diverse industries and invented several breakthrough products.

In 2001, Garry became active in the music industry in his role as a manager, concert promoter, and executive producer of several signed and unsigned artists. Calling on this experience, he launched Yellow Brick Road Entertainment in the fall of 2005 (a privately funded Web 2.0 interactive video startup) that targeted the music industry and led to the writing of this book.

He holds a Bachelor of Arts degree from DePaul University, as well as a CSS graduate degree from Harvard University (Finance and IT). He has been PMP certified since 2007 and is a Stanford Certified Project Manager (SCPM).

Garry has been married for thirty-five years to Mary Wheeler and has two daughters, Alyssa and Jillian. His hobbies and interests include abstract art, music, golf, softball, guitar, movies, home recording, racing stock cars, and traveling. He and Mary are active supporters of the Visual and Performing Arts in Southwest Florida, the Jimmy Fund and the Make-A-Wish Foundation.

After retiring in 2017, Garry and Mary sold their house, cars, furniture, etc. and traveled full-time around the world for almost three years.

They traveled to 73 countries until the pandemic hit. Garry has now been to over 100 countries in his lifetime.

Garry and Mary are in the process of releasing a book about their travels together called "Living Like You Mean It! - The Ultimate Guide to a Nomadic Lifestyle". The book will be published by Victory Independent Publishing, and it will be available on Amazon in the summer of 2024.

During the COVID pandemic, Garry returned to Florida and reinvented himself. He became a multi-award-winning international abstract artist and launched his art business late in 2020. You can view his work at www.gswheeler.com.

He also works with numerous arts related non-profit organizations and currently serves as the Board President of Marco Island Center for the Arts and the Art Center Theater in Marco Island, Florida.

Garry at his office at Yellow Brick Road Entertainment in 2006.

Garry with New Hampshire Governor John Lynch. Software Association 2006 Rookie of the Year Presentation

Garry in 2018

Garry in 2023

APPENDIX

EXHIBIT A

EXCERPTS FROM THE ORIGINAL BUSINESS PLAN EXECUTIVE SUMMARY SECTION (JANUARY 2006)

1.1 Business Opportunity

By capitalizing on the rapid adoption of video over broadband and wireless technologies, BandDigs will transform the relationship between bands and their fans by introducing a new subscription based web video community. Currently according to "SEO Music" there are over 700,000 bands on Myspace.com with 55 million users. iSound is projecting that they will have 600,000 bands on their site this year. Our site will offer bands like these the ability to communicate directly with their fan base using streaming and interactive desktop video on a global basis. BandDigs will also encourage fans to video chat about their favorite artists to friends and will serve as the catalyst to replace online text chatting with video chatting.

By capturing just a small % of the known bands on Myspace and related music professionals/small music related businesses (27,000 bands and 4,000 music professionals over the next 5 years) at $299 a year (including a camera the first year), and selling sponsorships/ advertising and related products/ services, BandDigs should easily generate revenues in excess of $15M in year 5. Currently, no other artist/music promotion site offers such a capability or service. Serving as a pioneer of this capability to the market by the end of April 2006 (Phase 1) should provide us with a competitive advantage for at least a brief period and should create quite a buzz in the industry.

We will also target larger corporate clients such as indie record labels, major record labels, terrestrial radio stations, management firms, larger promoters and venues. Corporate clients will be sold a packaged deal (branded page, cameras & training/set up), plus an annual subscription of between $499 and $999 depending on the size of the client. BandDigs will then serve as the corporate clients' video communication portal (outsourced model). Each artist on the site will still require a license to host chats even on the corporate clients' sites. Corporate clients will be offered the ability to resell BandDigs' subscription service and to run advertising on their landing page to offset the cost of their annual subscription.

Another objective will be to establish BandDigs as The Portal to other social networking sites (one click push through of video and other band promotional messages).

Lastly, we plan to monetize all aspects of the site capability (corporate sponsors, banner ads, sale of MPEG video and audio downloads ("Chatcasts"), ringtones and related band merchandise).

YBR Summary Strategy

- Complete the development and roll out the BandDigs site working with strategic partners by June 30th of 2006.
- Develop additional strategic alliances with technology companies to further enhance the artist and fan relationship and music experience (bolt-ons to BandDigs).

- Fully monetize the BandDigs site (pass through links for merch, CDs, digital downloads, ringtones & ticket sales). Sell video & audio "Chatcast" downloads of the chats on our site.
- Provide web marketing services to concert promoters and record labels.
- Sell corporate sponsorships (Band Video chats branded, "Chatcasts" downloads/ watermarks), banner ads on chat pages and on the website general pages.
- Acquire/integrate additional artist promotion websites over time.

1.2 Product/Service Description

BandDigs is a comprehensive web community, designed for bands/recording artists from all genres to talk directly to their fan base via streaming and interactive video. It will also provide a vehicle for their fans to talk to their friends interactively about the bands that they support via desktop video. Our primary objective is to transform the relationship between these bands and fans by pioneering the advancements in video technology & proliferation of broadband connections on a global basis. We also want to fully enable the fan base to promote their favorite artists on a broad scale in a fun and creative way.

The site will be sold on a subscription basis to the artists and be offered free to registered users. Artists will be able to recover the cost of their subscription by accommodating advertising (flash and banner ads) on their live chat pages. The artists will receive a commission on all advertising related to their chats, a % of the pay per view charges if applicable for their chats/streaming broadcast as well as commissions on their MPEG videos and digital downloads ("Chatcasts") sold on the BandDigs site. They will also be given a 20% commission on any new subscribers that they bring to the table.

Looking at our site from a bands' perspective, here is a conservative P & L for a band. This is a huge differentiator for our site. Bands can actually make good money while they build a much needed fan base. This analysis assumes that a band will run at least two chats per month with 50 participants on each one.

Projected Band Income (Year 1)
Advertising = $60
Merchandise sales (profit only) = $600
Pay per view fees = $180
Chatcast sales = $240
Referral sales commission = $60
Total Revenue = $1,140
Expenses
Merchandise = $200
BandDigs Subscription = $299
Total Expenses = $499
Net Profit = $641

Moreover, recognizing the rapid growth of web social communities such as Myspace, Friendster, Facebook and others, we have constructed BandDigs to serve as a portal to these other sites. In other words, we have made it very easy for a user on BandDigs to push BLOGs and video directly to other sites that they are registered on. The user simply creates one message about the band that they want to endorse and pushes the message out to a host of other BLOGGing sites. Our strategy with the site is to be open and seamless for all other sites to work with by embracing RSS (Really Simple Syndication).

Subsequently, our web community has been constructed in such a way to encourage fans to promote their favorite artists in a variety of different ways. Fans will be compensated for the level of support that they provide to their favorite artists.

FROM FAILURE TO FORTUNE

EXHIBIT B- SLIDES USED WITH EARLY POTENTIAL INVESTORS

Mission

- To revolutionize the online relationship between recording artists and their fans!

BandDigs Vision

- Leverage video technology for 1000's of bands to establish and maintain a more personal connection with their fan base (leading to band loyalty and promotional support).
- Help millions of music fans to satisfy their appetite for getting to know their favorite artists better and for telling others about them.

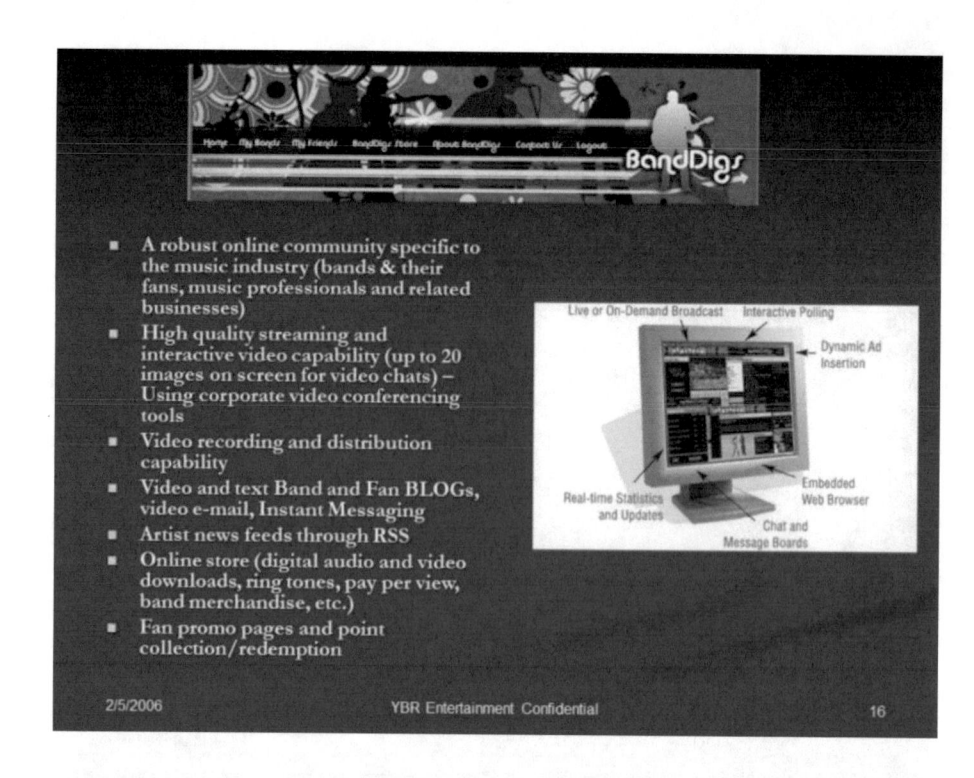

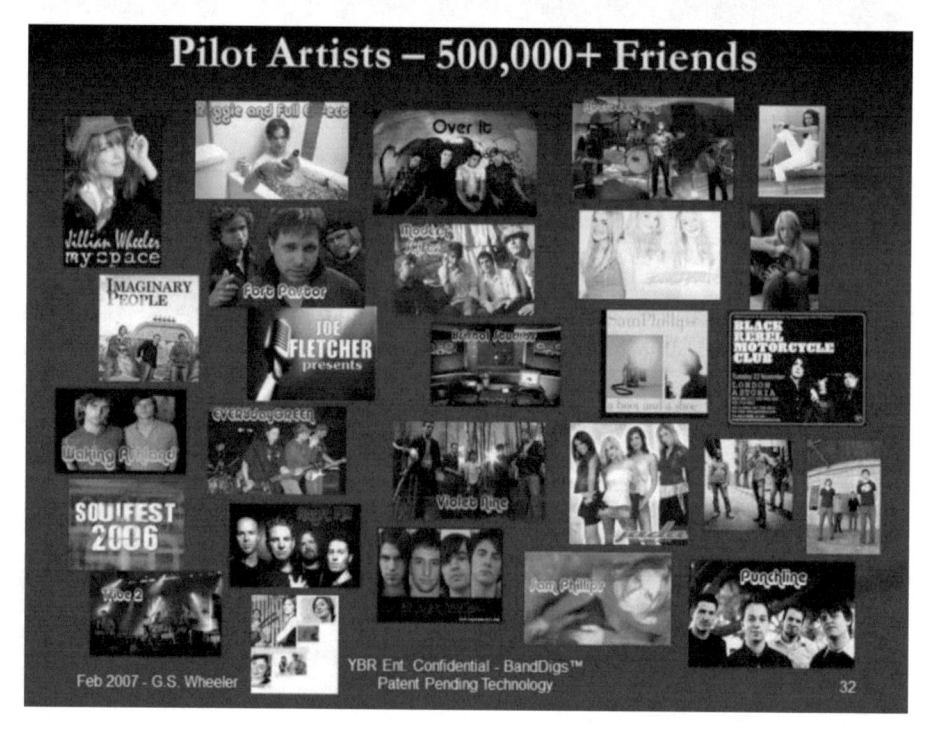

- A robust online community specific to the music industry (bands & their fans, music professionals and related businesses)
- High quality streaming and interactive video capability (up to 20 images on screen for video chats) – Using corporate video conferencing tools
- Video recording and distribution capability
- Video and text Band and Fan BLOGs, video e-mail, Instant Messaging
- Artist news feeds through RSS
- Online store (digital audio and video downloads, ring tones, pay per view, band merchandise, etc.)
- Fan promo pages and point collection/redemption

FROM FAILURE TO FORTUNE 155

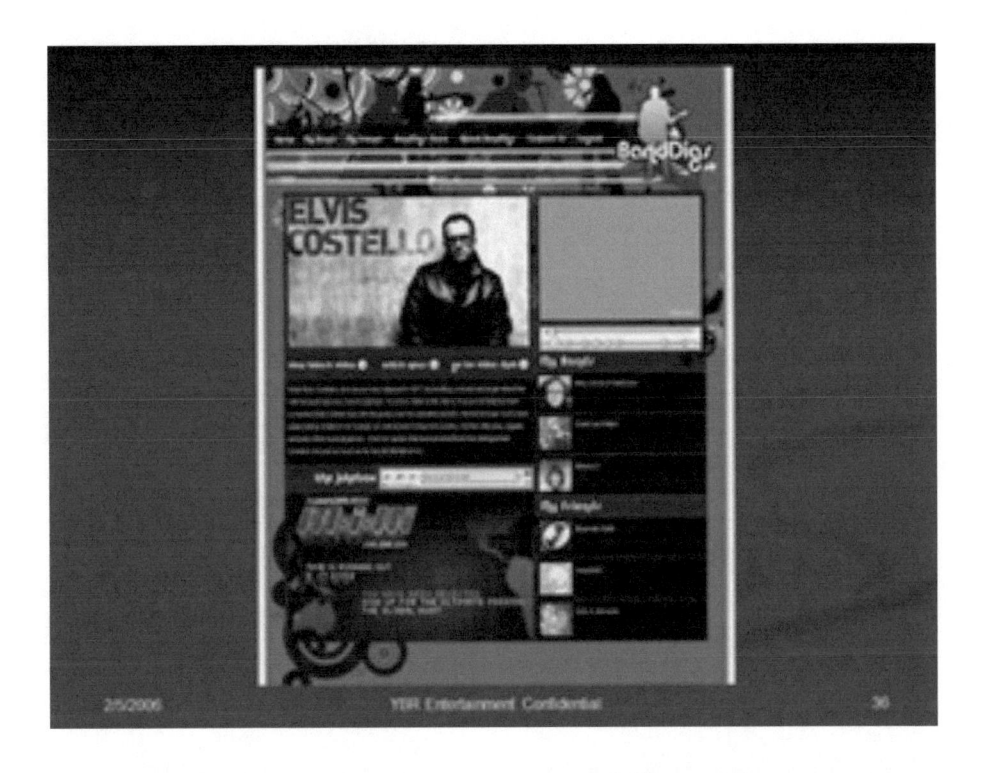

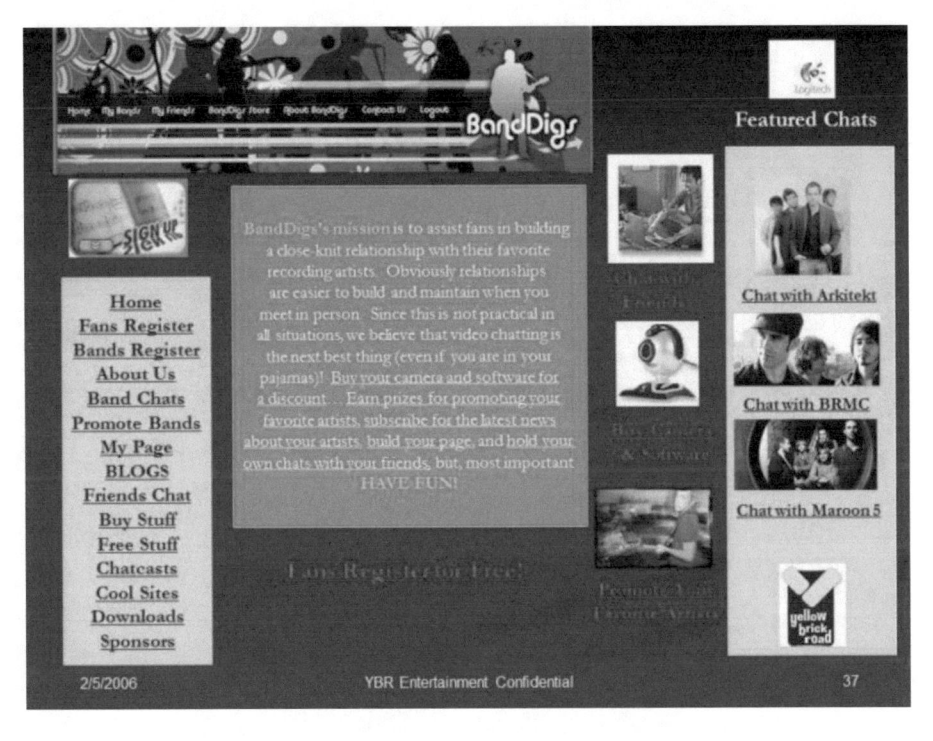

BandDigs
A Hyundai like you've never seen befo
AZER
Enter For A Chance To Win The All-New Hyundai Az
BUY MERCHENDIZE
VIDEO BLOG
BUY CHATCAST
JOIN FAN CLUB
CHAT
VIDEO CHAT WITH
Brought to you By
Hyundai
Jillian Wheeler
BEAUTIFUL THINGS

BandDigs
A Hyundai like you've never seen befo
AZER
Enter For A Chance To Win The All-New Hyundai Az
what is your favorite song ?
Sky is falling
Real Life
Disappearing
Vote Now!
View Results
What is your favorite song ?
Votes Ratio
Sky is falling 83 32%
Real Life 82 31%
Disappearing 98 37%
263 votes total
BUY MERCHENDIZE
VIDEO BLOG
BUY CHATCAST
JOIN FAN CLUB
CHAT

What Can the Artist Do?

- Talk to all fans one way with streaming video (webcasting and phonecasting)
- Enable (TBD) number of fans to interactively communicate via video
- Enable all fans to communicate interactively through polling/voting & text messaging
- Promote personal causes (earn $ for causes)
- Respond to questions and polling results collected during the session
- Ask fans to tell them more about themselves through chatting and polling
- Ask fans for input on latest song/CD, CD artwork, concert, video, etc.
- Establish a stronger relationship with fan base
- Understand more about their audience (profiling)
- Speak to the media, radio stations, fans, management, etc. while on the road
- Upload their current fan base e-mails and keep the e-mail lists of registered fans from BandDigs chats
- Choose from a list of BandDigs sponsors and earn $ from sponsorships
- Earn $ from fans participation on the chats
- Earn $ from selling subscriptions to other artists
- Earn $ from selling MPEGs/"Chatcasts"/merchandise/ringtones

What Can the Fan Do?

- Get to know their favorite artists better (establish a personal relationship)
- Support their favorite artists and their causes (% of their fees will go to the artist and the charity)
- Listen to new songs and see new video not available to the general public
- Have some influence over the artist's choices and career direction
- Promote artists with network of friends
- Subscribe to news and announcements in one place for multiple artists vs. going to artist's website
- Conveniently join fan clubs and find out automatically when a new song, CD, video is being released and when a band will be performing in the area
- Win prizes for participating in polling events
- Win prizes for promoting artists
- Buy keepsakes of their meeting with the band e.g. screen print, MPEG, "Chatcast"...
- Send playlists of favorites to others
- Earn "power promoter" status on the site recognized by Icons like EBay power sellers

Monetizing

- Sponsor banner ads/messages on "Chatcasts", etc. (tailored to each artist)
- Monthly/annual subscription fees for bands & corporate clients to use the site/infrastructure
- Monthly/annual subscriptions for fans to use premium services on the site (base access will be free)
- Sponsorships and advertising sold before and during live chats and on pages
- Band Chat Fees/Pay per event (for well known in demand artists)
- Software & Camera sales (low end and high end packages, sold individually or in discounted bundles)
- MPEG video and "Chatcasts" of the chats (prove to your friends you were online with your favorite artist) – Take it with you on your video iPod
- Print screen capability (framed copy of your photo on screen with your favorite artist)
- Band collectibles/autographed items (commissions) – package with premium chats
- Pass through links to digital downloads, merchandise, CDs, videos, concert tickets, for sale on partner sites, etc.
- Concert and record promotion fees to local promoters and/or venues & record labels
- Custom skins (design your own theme)
- Webinars (how to use video and other topics)

EXHIBIT C

YELLOW BRICK ROAD ENTERTAINMENT LLC

NON-BINDING TERM SHEET
FOR SEED FINANCING

Preamble: The intent of this Non-Binding Term Sheet is to set forth the terms pursuant to which the undersigned Investor(s) would purchase Convertible Debentures from Yellow Brick Road Entertainment LLC ("YBR"). This is not, and is not intended to be, an offer to sell securities.

Parties:	The undersigned Investors (collectively the "Investors") would provide financing to YBR. All of the Investors shall be "accredited investors," as defined in Rule 501 of Regulation D..
Amount:	Up to a total of $600,000, with a minimum investment per Investor of at least $50,000.
Structure:	Unsecured convertible debentures, 10% annual interest rate, payable two (2) years from Closing ("Seed Notes"). Upon conversion, the accrued interest shall be payable in cash, unless the Investor and YBR otherwise agree and except as provided in the "Warrant" paragraph below. No principal or interest shall be due until the maturity date of the Seed Notes.
Conversion:	The unpaid principal amount of all of the Seed Notes shall convert into an equivalent amount of preferred stock upon the same terms as YBR's next round of equity financing that raises gross proceeds of at least $1,000,000 ("Qualifying A Round") prior to the maturity date of the Seed Notes. Investors may elect to waive this Qualifying A Round threshold.

Warrant:	At the time that Seed Notes are issued, the Seed Investors shall receive Warrants to purchase a total number of shares of common stock of the Corporation equal to 10% of the then issued and outstanding shares of common stock of the Corporation (after taking into account the shares issuable upon exercise of the Warrants). The exercise price shall be the total principal and accrued interest of the Seed Notes. The Warrants shall automatically be exercised on the maturity date of the Seed Notes only if on such date the Seed Notes have not been converted as set forth above. In the event that the Seed Notes are converted upon the consummation of the Qualifying A Round, the Warrants shall automatically expire. On the maturity date of the Seed Notes, if the Seed Notes have not been converted, then the Seed Notes shall be deemed to be payment of the exercise price of the Warrants and the Corporation shall issue to the Investors the shares of common stock issuable upon exercise of the Warrants.
Discount:	If the Seed Notes are converted upon the closing of the Qualifying A Round, then the Seed Notes shall be converted into the number of shares of stock calculated by dividing (a) the then unpaid principal amount of the Seed Notes by (b) the an amount determined by multiplying the purchase price per share in the Qualifying A Round by 85%.
Use of Proceeds:	Working capital.
Transaction Documentation:	This term sheet shall serve as the basis for a Convertible Note, Note Purchase Agreement, and/or any other documents required to implement this term sheet's provisions.
Expenses:	Each party shall bear the expenses such party incurs to prepare, review, negotiate, and execute the legal documentation for this transaction.
Closing:	As soon as practicable.
Non-Binding:	This Term Sheet reflects the present intention of the Investors and YBR and does not, and is not intended to, create a legally binding agreement; the agreement of the parties, if any, would be reflected in definitive documentation that would be negotiated and be executed and delivered on behalf of all parties.

ACKNOWLEDGED AND ACCEPTED:

YBR:

YELLOW BRICK ROAD ENTERTAINMENT LLC

_____   _____
Garry Wheeler – Manager   Date

Investors:

_____   _____
Signature   Date

_____
Name (please print or type)

_____   _____
Signature   Date

_____   _____
Signature   Date

_____   _____
Signature   Date

EXHIBIT D

ORIGINAL FINANCIAL ASSUMPTIONS FROM THE BUSINESS PLAN

10.1 Assumptions

Below is a summary of the assumptions used to project the next 36 months of YBR's planned operation.

The software package that this plan was created in does not allow a 5 year projection. Years 4 and 5 have been included, but you will find them in a slightly different format compared to years 1 to 3. In addition, we have attached a separate set of slides summarizing all 5 years of the financials in Powerpoint format.

Beginning Balance Sheet

Cash - The amount of cash after the anticipated $400,000 infusion. Of this amount, $200,000 will be spent on finishing the development of BandDigs and on the initial marketing effort for the site. We start with $200,000 in working capital. The company will also maintain a $100,000 line of credit with Citizens Bank and will borrow $100,000 later in Year 1 to support the company's planned growth

Cash Summary

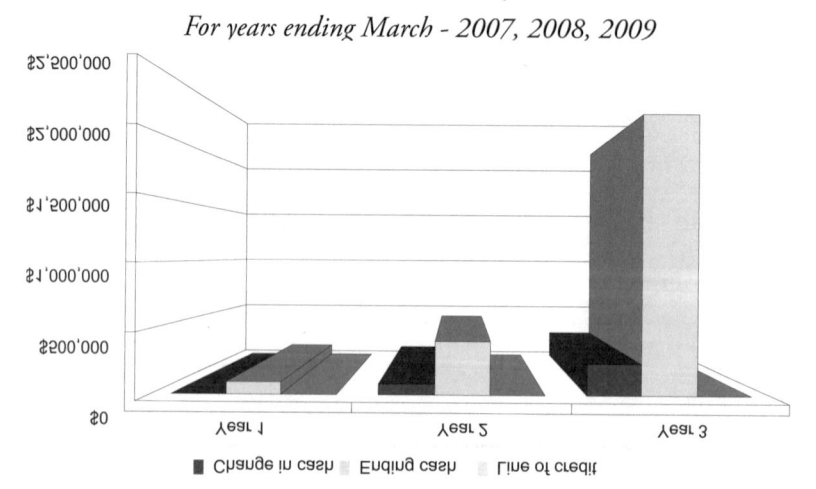

For years ending March – 2007, 2008, 2009

Inventory - We will not carry any inventory. The camera packages will be sold under a drop ship arrangement with Logitech.

Fixed assets (net) - Our fixed assets will include BandDigs, some computers for the infrastructure, HD camera equipment and office computers.

Total equity - This is anticipated joint investment by Garry Wheeler and the new equity partner(s), as well as the value of BandDigs

Profit & Loss

Profit & Loss

For years ending March - 2007, 2008, 2009

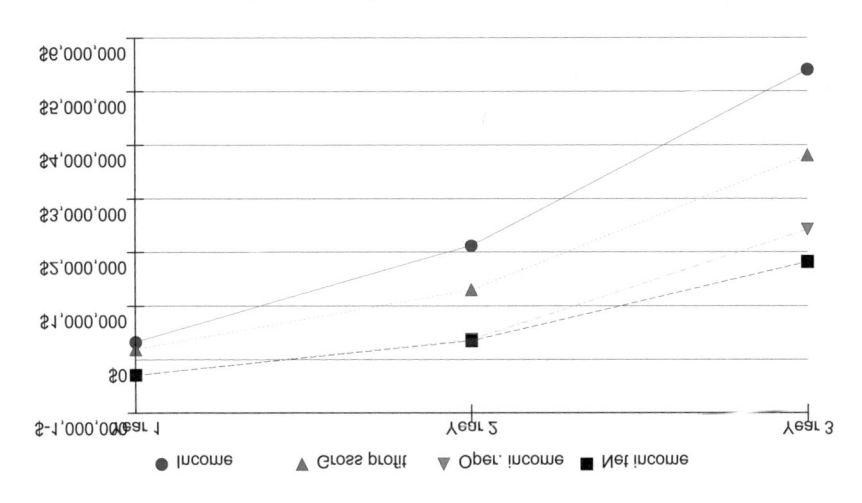

Income

Income by Category
For years ending March - 2007, 2008, 2009

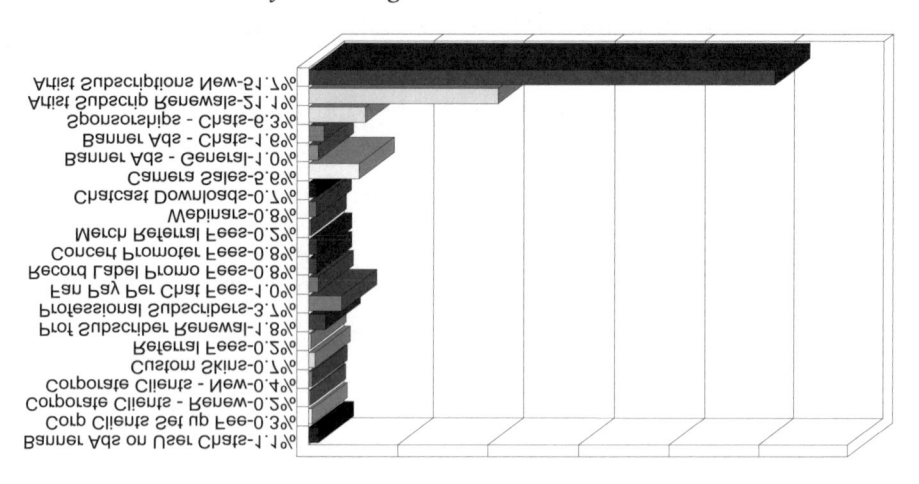

Category	%
Artist Subscriptions New	51.7%
Artist Subscrip Renewals	21.1%
Sponsorships - Chats	6.9%
Banner Ads - Chats	1.6%
Banner Ads - General	1.0%
Camera Sales	5.6%
Chatcast Download	0.7%
Webinars	0.8%
Merch Retail Fees	0.2%
Concert Promoter Fees	0.8%
Record Label Promo Fees	0.8%
Fan Pay Per Chat Fees	1.0%
Professional Subscribers	3.1%
Prof Subscriber Renewals	1.8%
Retail Fees	0.2%
Custom Skins	0.1%
Corporate Clients - New	0.4%
Corporate Clients - Renewal	0.2%
Corp Clients Set up Fee	0.3%
Banner Ads on User Chats	1.1%

Subscriptions (Bands & Professional Users)

Year 1 = 1,000, Year 2 = 5,500, Year 3 = 12,000, Year 4 = 21,00, Year 5 = 31,000

We assumed that we will have an 80% renewal rate of subscribers year over year

Subscriptions (Corporate)

Year 1 = 5, Year 2 = 25, Year 3 = 50, Year 4 = 75, Year 5 = 200

No Charge Registered Users (assumed that each new artist will bring 20 new fans with them to the site on average)

Year 1 = 45,000 (including pilot bands list), Year 2 = 100,000, Year 3 = 220,000, Year 4 = 380,000, Year 5 = 540,000

Live Chats (assumed each band will do 1 chat per month with their fan base, of which 5% will be considered premium chats and be sold as a pay per view event)

Year 1 = 10,200, Year 2 = 60,000, Year 3 = 132,000, Year 4 = 228,000, Year 5 = 324,000

Price for the premium pay per view chat = $9.95 to $19.99....

Price for one on one time/guaranteed face on the screen = $9.95

Advertisers

% of the chats will be branded by a corporate sponsor and have at least 1 banner ad running during the event

Year 1 = 10% (1,020) Year 2 = 40% (24,000), Year 3 = 50% (66,000), Year 4 = 60% (136,800), Year 5 = 75% (243,000)

Prices of ad space (branded page, watermark, podcast, flash video before chat) - Premium artist = $10-$25 (increasing $5 a year over the 5 years), Developing artist = $2.50 to $7.50 (increasing each year over the 5 years)

Prices of banner ad space on chats - Premium artist = $10-$15, Developing artist = $1, Fan Chats .50 in years 1 and 2 and $1 in year 3-5

% of new bands that will purchase a camera = 5%, Year 1, 15% years 2 and 3, 5% years 4 and 5

% of registered uses that will purchase a camera - Year 1 = 1%, Year 2 = 3% and Year 3 = 2%, Years 4 and 5 =1%

% of fans that will purchase a video of the chatcast from our site = 5% in year 1 and 10% years 2-5 at $1.99

% of users who will purchase band merchandise that we will earn a 10% commission on = 2% year 1, 5% in years 2 and 3 and 10% in years 4 and 5

% of bands who will purchase webinar training = 10% year 1, 15% in year 2, 20% years 3-5

Number of Concert promoter packages sold - Year 1 = 4, Year 2 = 25, Year 3 = 100, Year 4 = 150, Year 5 = 250

Number of Record Label promo packages sold - Year 1 = 4, Year 2 = 25, Year 3 =100, Year 4 = 150, Year 5 = 250

% of bands who will want a custom landing page created - Year 1 = 2%, Year 2 = 4%, Years 3 to 5 = 3%

COGS

For the first time subscribers, YBR must pay a royalty to Inept Solutions for the product development. This royalty payment starts out as high as $35.00 for the first 1000 subscribers and declines to $7.99 for 50,000 and above. The royalty discounts for hitting the threshold show up as a credit in our expenses (see below). We have estimated that our concurrent users will run at 20% of the subscribers.

For the first year subscribers, we will be shipping them a $39 Web-Cam as part of their subscription fee.

We have assumed that 50% of all subscriptions will be sold by our partners and they will earn a 20% on all subscriptions sold (so a 10% line item has been built into the COGs).

We will kick back 20% of all advertising $ to the bands for allowing the ads to take place on their chats. We will also match what the band chooses to allocate to their favorite charity/cause up to 5% of the advertising $ collected.

We will pay a 10% commission on all ads generated to outside sales people.

For cameras, we assumed a 10% margin for the referral to Logitech and their drop ship. ($89 price to bands and $39 to fans).

Expense Projection

For years ending March - 2007, 2008, 2009

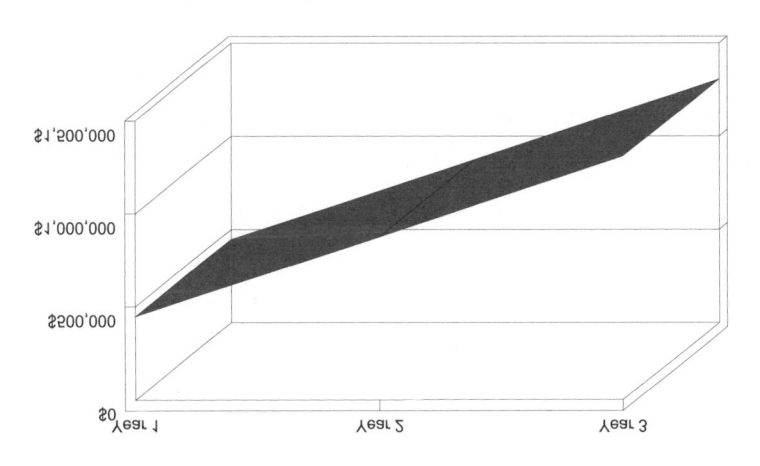

Expenses by Category

For years ending March - 2007, 2008, 2009

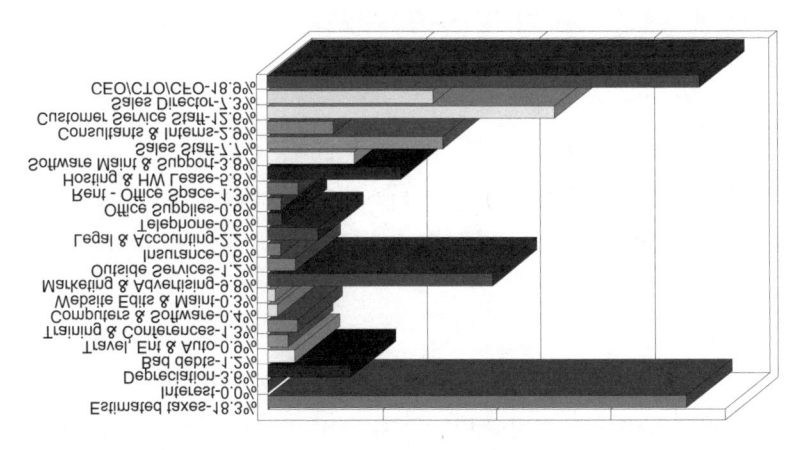

Advertising - Monthly advertising for BandDigs will run ~$10,000 a month in year 1, ~$8,000 a month in year 2 and $15,000 a month in year 3, $20,000 in year 4 and $25,000 in year 5

Insurance - YBR will maintain business and product liability insurance. The average annual cost of coverage will be $6,000.

Legal & accounting - Legal and accounting expenses assume fixed monthly retainers for YBR's legal counsel and accountants.

Marketing personnel - YBR plans to hire one full-time individual for the last six months of year one at a base of $4,000 per month. Two additional marketing personnel will be added at the beginning of year two. A payroll burden of 25 percent has been added to cover taxes and benefits.

Rent - For the first year, the company will rent the existing space in Garry Wheeler's home allocated for YBR for $600 per month. The space can comfortably handle the first year's growth and the space is less expensive than commercial space would be and there are only minor fit up costs. Year 2, we will fit up office space and pay market rates

Research & development - Our second release of BandDigs will be 15-18 months after the current release and another release will occur at the 24 month mark.

Royalty Rebate - To simplify the financial's, we added a line item titled "Royalty Rebate" which is shown as a credit to expenses. We calculated the rebate due for hitting certain thresholds (number of first time subscribers) with Inept Solutions

Salaries (Owners/Asst.) - Garry Wheeler will earn a salary of $100,000 the first year. In years 2 and 3 his salary will be increased to market rates.

YBR will hire a Customer Service Manager in Q1 of Year 1 for $60,000 and a sales & marketing director for $90,000 in Q4 of Year 1. 1 part time sales person will be hired right away to help in selling advertising and subscriptions. 1 Customer Service Rep will be hired at $40,000 toward the end of the first year and a second will be added 6 months later. A payroll burden of 25 percent has been added to cover taxes and benefits. YBR will also continue to use college interns and outside service providers to help as required.

Software Maint, Support, Website Hosting - BandDigs will be hosted and maintained by Inept Solutions and SAVVIS communications. We will also pay for call center support in Nashville, TN.

Training & Conferences - These funds will be used for YBR personnel to attend several regional and national tradeshows. This monthly amount does not include travel, which is listed separately.

Travel - These funds will enable YBR personnel to visit and train new customers as well as attend trade shows.

Depreciation - Depreciation is calculated on a straight-line method based upon the associated life of YBR's assets. Computers and telephones are depreciated over 5 years, office furniture is depreciated over 7 years, manufacturing equipment is depreciated over 5 years, and building improvements are depreciated over 39 years.

Interest expense - YBR will pay 8% on any cash borrowed from our credit line & 10% on the $100,000 borrowed in Year 1.

Estimated taxes - The annual amount estimated to cover taxes is calculated at an average percent of 25 percent of net income before taxes. This amount is computed on a monthly basis.

Balance Sheet

Financial Position

For years ending March - 2007, 2008, 2009

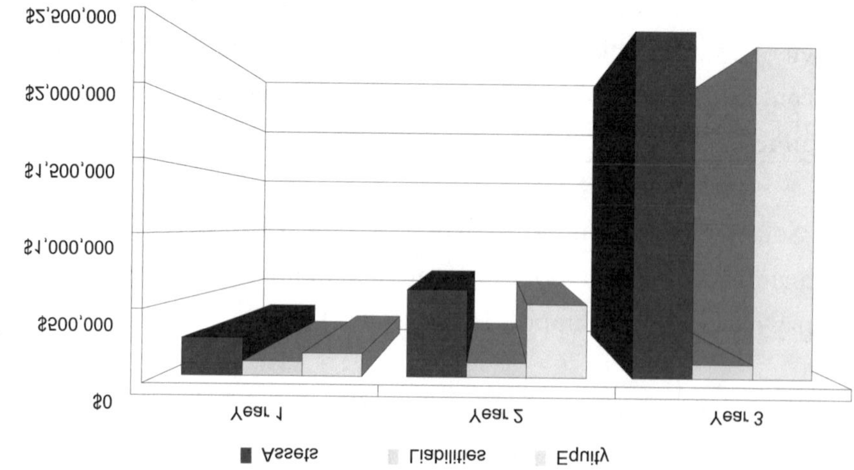
$2,500,000
$2,000,000
$1,500,000
$1,000,000
$500,000
$0
Year 1
Year 2
Year 3
Assets
Liabilities
Equity

Accounts receivable (net) - All of BandDigs's subscription related services will be paid for upfront (mostly through credit cards). The advertising will be sold on 30 day payable terms. 2% will not be paid for some reason.

Inventory - YBR will not carry inventory.

Fixed assets (net) - This is the value of YBR's equipment net of depreciation.

Line of credit - YBR's line of credit will be needed in year 2.

Cash Plan

Break-even Income Analysis

For years ending March - 2007, 2008, 2009

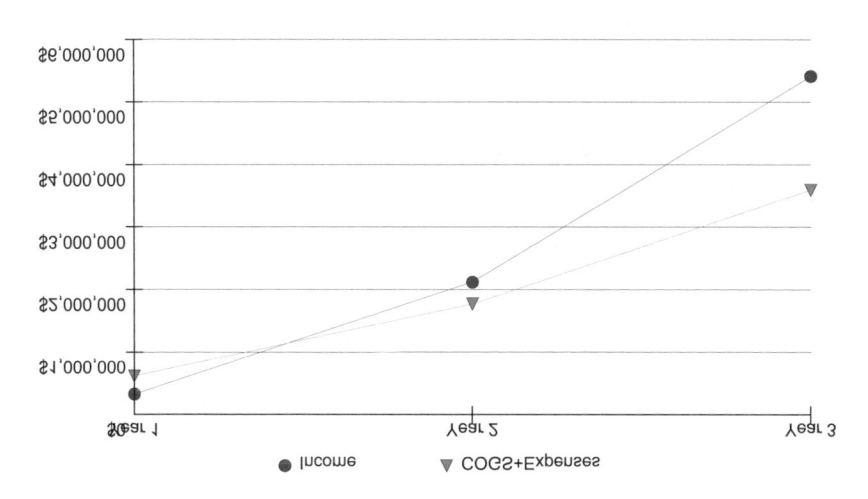

```
$6,000,000
$5,000,000
$4,000,000
$3,000,000
$2,000,000
$1,000,000
            Year 1           Year 2           Year 3
         ● Income    ▼ COGS+Expenses
```

Cash receipts - Sales of advertising to customers will be made on Net 30 credit terms. The forecast assumes that cash will be received in the month following the sale. Due to the nature of YBR's target market, a 2% bad debt figure was used.

Other costs of sales - 20% of advertising $ will be kicked back to bands. 10% of all sales will be paid in outside commissions. 3% will be paid to the credit card companies.

Issuance of debt - In Year 1, YBR plans to secure a credit line with Citizens bank of $100,000 and in Year 2 (mid year), plans to borrow an additional $100,000 to support the company's planned growth.

Interest payments - Please refer to "Interest expense" in the Profit & Loss assumptions section.

Line of credit activity - As required for cash flow purposes.

EXHIBIT E

High Level BandDigs Deliverables

General requirement:

- Registration for Bands, Fans, Corporate
- The site and registration and function process will comply with COPPA laws
- Enable video e-mail (pre-record a promotional message and send it out to your registered users, fan club, etc.)
- Enable video instant messaging to AOL, MSN, Yahoo, Skype…. Compactable with other IM or have a separate BandDigs instant message
- Robust (search capability)

Bands Section

- Customized BandDigs page and brand their own chat page
- Allow the band to select from multiple templates for their pages. For an additional fee, we will design them a custom page
- Branded media player for bands and corporate clients on a fee basis
- Ad management and integration on all pages of the band
- Digital rights and digital rights management of the band IP
- Promote personal causes on the site in the artist branding area. Designate a % of advertising and/or merchandise sales to go the nonprofit of their choice.

Email

- Easily import the bands e-mail mailing list to BandDigs and automatically create an account for the userband. BandiDigs will then notify the fan that the band has authorized them to join their fan club on BandDigs. Only verification of their email is required to join the community. A registration page on BandDigs will ask to be filled out to provide additional information
- Send out chat notifications (via e-mail, instant messaging and text messaging) to their fan base and ask them to register.
- Use the site to speak to members of the media and/or their sponsors, managers, agents, radio stations, promoters, venues, etc.
- Create and publish a photo library on their page using Flicker API not unlimited galleries
- Seamless links to their own website, Sonic Bids EPK, Myspace account, CD Baby, other artist promotion sites (no restrictions). These other pages will open on another browser
- Podcast subscriptions through RSS (Podcasts may be offered by the bands, sponsors, corporate clients and/or fans)
- Collect artist news using RSS from a variety of news sources and publish info automatically on the band's pages

Video Application

- Multiple video chat capability
- Compatibility with Mac and PC
- Enable the use of DV cameras so that the bands can broadcast a higher quality video stream of the rehearsals, showcase, recording session etc, by plugging in their camera on a tripod for the broadcast

- Talk to fans one way with streaming video in large numbers (webcasting & phone casting). No audience size limits
- Allow streaming video fan participants to provide feedback through polling feature and text messaging
- Pre-record short e-mail/instant messaging videos and send them to their registered fan base

Video Chat

- All video chats to be recorded so that video and audio recordings can be sold after the chat is completed. The watermark chat with BandDigs along with the advertising
- Up to 20 simultaneous interactive people on a chat, but be able to control the number (set it up before the chat occurs 5 to 50 users to be displayed on the screen)
- Raise the hand functionality to put people in a que to ask their question (in priority order)
- One on one chatting capability… The intent is that a fan can pay extra to get one on one time with the artist and we can package this chat along with signed merchandise and sell it as a line item. The host and the participant image will join together as larger images in the middle of the screen like Apple's i-chat.
- Ability to feature artists and upcoming chats on the BandDigs home page (fee based)
- Allow the artist to prerecord a message for their chat page that will run before the advertising (welcoming their fans to the chat)
- Allow the band to post their own videos and songs to their pages
- Enable up to 50 concurrent users initially to participate in interactive chats with up to 10 images on the screen at the same time; 5 fans pictures on the screen will be cycled through during the

chat every few minutes. We want to be able to lock in someone's space on the screen on a fee basis.

- The host should retain the right to terminate someone's participation on a chat as they deem appropriate (drop the caller, block the caller, etc.)
- The artist should pre-approve all participants on the call. The fans must first register for an account on BandDigs and then register for participation in the specific chats
- The artist must pre-approve the ads that will run on their chat pages
- Chat/training sessions, bands can chat one on one on the screen. Ideal for instrumental lessons.

Phone

- Compatibility with Verizon Vcast and other phone video

Blogs

- Copy paste capability of BLOG data to other sites. – Syndication and RSS feed
- Creation of Blogs about their fans and or concerts.

Reports & Tracking:

- Track and report the advertising done on each specific artist chat page
- Ability to ask fans to participate in real time polling and/or after the fact polling

- Track all of the fans that are members of their BandDigs fan club. We will provide the band with the user registration data and e-mail info
- Profile their audience, so after fans register for a chat with the artist, the artist will be able to run a report to get demographic data about all of the registered participants on the call
- Track/report statistics related to their fan base
- Display top 10 artist (Band Ratings), on the home page and other ranking as define later in the business rule.

Fans Section

- Register on the site providing only the required information under COPPA laws.
- Register for free chats with the bands
- Create and publish a photo library on their page using Flickr API
- Receive traditional e-mail alerts, video e-mails, podcasts, latest news etc. from the band by requesting notifications through RSS
- Join fan clubs on BandDigs and back on the artist's site
- Participate in streaming video broadcasts and provide feedback through polling and/or text messaging
- Build their own band promotions page and chat page (selecting from several design templates)
- Pull down help menus (how to set up your camera, how to conduct a chat, questions to ask the band, etc.)
- Calendar: a master schedule where the fans can view by genre the types of chats that are planned for the day, week or month. The calendar would show Live show; Backstage chats; Recording Sessions; Rehearsals; Meet and Greet; Showcases; Contest; Band Review session; Jam session and Training session.

Video Chats

- Participate in free video chats with the bands
- Watch band videos and listen to songs for free
- Download free (pre-authorized by bands and/or sponsors) videos, podcasts and songs
- Add seating charts according to the priority that is defined.
- One on One chat with 2 video screens with only

Chat recordings

Download Chat casts for a fee to I-Tunes/I-Pods, approved phones and other video on demand devices (this download functionality will need to be robust)

E Commerce

- E commerce and e pay
- Pay pal integration
- MS Commerce server integration

Ad Manager

- Integration for Video & Banner Ads
- Reports and Ad Management

Blogs

- BLOG the artists and/or BLOG to friends about the artist. Create video BLOGs for the band members. Push your BLOG entries to other sites that they have login credentials on e.g. Myspace, Facebook, Live Journal, Xanga, etc.

Search

Add a robust search functionality as the Bands/ Fans/ Video/ etc to be defined as per the business rules

Reports & Tracking:

- ➢ Ability to track points earned by fans on BandDigs for specific promoting activities that they do to support a band e.g. they will earn points for the chats that they participate in, the merchandise that they buy from the artist, the number of new fans that they attract to the BandDigs site, the creation of a BandDigs fan page that has the artist listed on it, the amount of BLOGGing that they do in support of the band, etc. These points will need to be tracked and maintained in the user's account so that they can use the points to redeem prizes from the bands that they support
- ➢ Ability to use the tracking feature for the time used by the Artist and other users and give a graphical representation for the usage per month as the business rule defines.
- ➢ Earn points for promoting their favorite artists which will be redeemable later for prizes (earn points for getting more fans to sign up to help the artist, for participating in chats and polls and from buying band merchandise, etc.)
- ➢ Send playlists of favorites to other registered users on the site or to people outside BandDigs via e-mail
- ➢ Earn "Power" Promoter status on the site recognized by Icons similar to Ebay's power sellers

Professional Section

- Registration page (see this section)
- Create their own branded BandDigs page/chat page
- Clients must pre-approve all advertising done on their pages. They may decline to have advertising on their page. If they allow it, they will be compensated for it
- Upload and Run their own advertising and/or sponsor messages on their chat page
- Promote their own artists and/or services
- Conduct training webinars using polling features, application sharing, raise the hand, etc.
- Branded media player Professionals on a fee basis

Corporate Section

- Create their own branded BandDigs corporate page/chat page
- Upload their logo or link to external sites
- Highlights of their services
- Promote their own artists and/or services
- Conduct training webinars using polling features, application sharing, raise the hand, etc.
- Branded media player corporate clients on a fee basis

Video

- Conduct streaming and interactive video chats with their registered user base to include, employees, vendors, fans, artists, sponsors, business partners, media, etc.
- Offer free video, audio downloads and podcasts

Schedule & Calendar

- ➤ Conduct streaming and interactive video chats and schedule the chat session.
- ➤ Schedule in their personal calendar what are the new events coming up
- ➤ Other schedule for the bands and corporate for announcements

Reports & Tracking

- ➤ Track and report user participation
- ➤ Set time limits for streaming chat time and interactive chat time for the month. Report on how much time has been used so far by user/ user type

High Level Development Schedule that Inept Solutions Proposed

Project launch: April 17, 2006

Network Set up: May 26, 2006

- MS Commerce Server
- Video Server

Application Development: May 26, 2006

- Portal and other applications
- Media server & encoder

Testing of application phase 1: June 6, 2006

Testing beta application phase 2: June 13, 2006

Testing final changes: June 23, 2006

Go Live: June 23, 2006

EXHIBIT F

BandDigs.com Terms of Pilot Artist/Pilot Business Offer

Yellow Brick Road Entertainment, LLC with a place of business at PO Box 467, Windham, NH ("Us", "We", "YBR") is pleased to offer _____ with a place of business at _____ ("Participant", "You") the opportunity to play a part as one of the pilot participants (artists/ bands/music related business) of BandDigs.com. This memo sets forth the material terms and conditions of the agreement between YBR and You (the "Agreement") with respect to the BandDigs Pilot Artist/Pilot Business Program.

Please fill out the registration form (link to be provided to you by YBR).

This Agreement is incorporated into and is subject to the BandDigs Terms and Conditions.

You understand and agree that YBR is the sole and exclusive owner of certain confidential information ("Confidential Information") and intellectual property rights collectively entitled "BandDigs", (collectively "Properties") and You agree to keep in strictest confidence, and not to disclose or divulge or use any Confidential Information, except as directed by Us.

Participant (You) will receive, FREE-OF-CHARGE:

- The use of the BandDigs site and entitlement to receive all of the benefits associated with BandDigs paying artist or small business subscribers for as long as BandDigs offers such subscriptions;
- Featured space on the BandDigs site during the first few months of the site launch;
- Participation in the BandDigs referral program, in which You will receive 20% of the initial subscription fees paid to BandDigs by any artist referred to BandDigs by You

- Participation in the BandDigs advertising program, in which You will receive 20% of net advertising revenue paid to BandDigs in connection with advertising specific to Your site or content (which advertising is subject to Your approval);

- Participation in the BandDigs publication program, in which You will receive an "all-in" royalty of 50% of the net revenue received by BandDigs from BandDigs' reuse of Your posted BandDigs Content (which reuse is subject to Your approval);

- The opportunity to provide feedback and suggest future enhancements;

- Promo page preparation including the creation of a flash banner, template and the uploading of the basic content;

- Training on how to use the video chat capability and assistance during Your first video chats;

- Promotional banners to be used on Your website, Myspace and other sites;

- A webcam if You need one (e.g., a Logitech Quickcam or Mac iSight) at no charge to You. Tell Us if You need a webcam as soon as possible and where You would like it to be delivered;

- Assistance in editing and encoding Your first BandDigs promotional videos should You need it. In some cases, We may also offer to record Your BandDigs promo video (time and travel permitting);

- Inclusion in our PR campaign;

- Training as required to support You during the early phases of the site launch

In return, you grant Us the right to use Your names, likenesses, trademarks, and approved biographical materials for advertising or promoting

BandDigs or its services, including on any websites operated or owned by YBR, and to fully cooperate with Us and render best efforts to:

- Assist Us in testing and debugging the site with particular emphasis on Your own promotion pages and video chat capabilities;
- Help Us with the launching of the site, including by sending out invitations to join the BandDigs community and to participate in Your video chats to Your fans (e.g., all of Your Myspace friends and Your own e-mail list). Note: We will help You to import Your e-mail list so that You can send out an invitation from Your BandDigs account directly;
- Promote BandDigs to Your fan/customer base on an ongoing basis e.g. forwarding press releases, press coverage, etc. if appropriate
- Record a short BandDigs promo video that You can also use to e-mail Your fans inviting them to join and a "Welcome to my BandDigs" video for Your promo page
- Provide Us with content for Your promotional page as required;
- Conduct an agreed-upon number of video chats with our assistance and provide Us with Your feedback and suggestions
- Post our logo/link on Your website and on Your Myspace page if possible
- Serve as a customer reference (provided that You are happy with Your BandDigs experience)

Each party reserves the right to terminate this Agreement upon 30 days written notice in the event of an uncured material breach of the terms and conditions of this Agreement.

Authorization: The individual executing this agreement on behalf of a corporation or other legal entity personally represents that he or she is duly authorized to execute this Agreement on behalf of such entity and that this Agreement is binding upon such entity.

EXHIBIT G

ACCREDITED INVESTOR CERTIFICATION

The undersigned, in connection with his/her/its contemplated investment in and purchase of units (the "Units") of Yellow Brick Road Entertainment LLC, a New Hampshire limited liability company (the "Company"), makes the following representations to the Company, recognizing that the Company is relying on these representations in connection with its claim for exemption from registrations under applicable federal and state securities laws for the offer and any sale of Units to the undersigned:

(a) that he/she/it qualifies as an "accredited investor", as that term is used in Regulation D promulgated under the Securities Act of 1933 (the "Act"), because **(check one)**:

(1) ____ it is a savings and loan association or other institution specified in Section 3(a)(5)(A) of the Act;

(2) ____ it is a private business development company as defined in Section 202(a)(22) of the Investment Advisers Act of 1940;

(3) ____ it is an organization described in Section 501(c)(3) of the Internal Revenue Code, a corporation, a Massachusetts or similar business trust, or a partnership, not formed for the specific purpose of acquiring the securities offered, with total assets in excess of $5,000,000;

(4) ____ he/she is a director, executive officer, or general partner of the Company;

(5) ____ he/she is an individual who has an individual net worth, or joint net worth with his or her spouse, in excess of $1,000,000;

(6) ____ he/she is an individual who had an income in excess of $200,000 in each of the two most recent years or joint income with his or her spouse in excess of $300,000 in each of those years and who reasonably expects to reach the same income level in the current year;

(7) ____ it is a trust with total assets in excess of $5,000,000, not formed for the specific purpose of acquiring the securities being offered, whose purchase is directed by a sophisticated person as described in Rule 506(b)(2)(ii) under the Act; or

(8) ____ it is an entity, all of whose equity owners are accredited investors.

(b) that he/she/it/they is/are a resident of the State/Commonwealth of _____.

EXHIBIT H

EXEC SUMMARY USED WITH VCs AND ANGELS

Yellow Brick Road Entertainment
An exciting opportunity in interactive video & digital community promotion solutions for the entertainment industry

Yellow Brick Road Entertainment (YBR) is a new venture focused on creating and applying technology solutions that revolutionize the relationship between celebrities and their fan base The company is seeking $4,000,000 in equity financing (Series A) to support its recent launch of an award winning and first of its kind web based video application suite and comprehensive digital community www.BandDigs.com for the music industry and the subsequent build out for all types of celebrities e.g. sports, actors, authors, etc.. With the help of $600,000 in seed round funding from angel investors, YBR completed the site/software development work, built its baseline team, engaged 50 pilot artists/businesses in its beta testing and released the 1.0 site.

At the helm of the YBR is Garry Wheeler (President/CEO), a music industry savvy information technology veteran and successful entrepreneur, along with a prominent group of entertainment industry Advisors. Garry's 30 year career has included executive roles (IT and GM) with many prominent high-tech companies. He was also the Founder/President of Align-IT & Design One Development. As a co-founder/Principal of Granite Rocks Records, he has served as an Artist Manager and Executive Producer for the last 5 years and has been very active in artist promotion and fan base development. He is a graduate of DePaul University and Harvard University.

FROM FAILURE TO FORTUNE 187

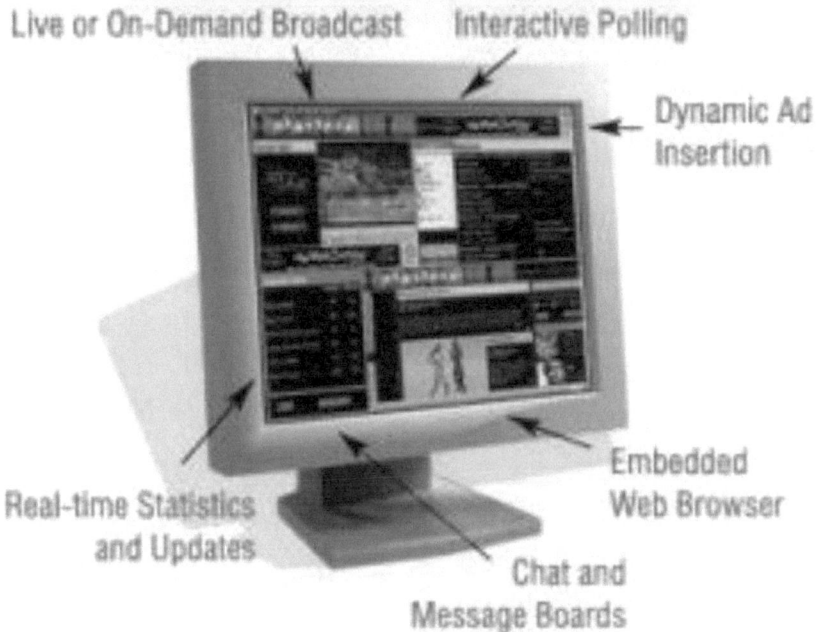

Live or On-Demand Broadcast   Interactive Polling

Dynamic Ad Insertion

Real-time Statistics and Updates

Chat and Message Boards

Embedded Web Browser

Opportunity:

- Capitalizing on the rapid adoption of video over broadband and online social communities, **BandDigs (a breakthrough interactive video community) is revolutionizing the relationship between celebrities and their fans.** There are over 4 million bands listed on Myspace.com alone (our initial target market). Our site offers bands and other celebrities the ability to communicate directly with their fan base using interactive desktop video on a global basis. **BandDigs** also provides subscribers with a streaming video broadcast tool that allows them to broadcast live video over the Internet from their rehearsal spaces, studios, venues, homes, offices, etc. at any time they wish.

- By allowing bands and fans to subscribe for free initially, we believe we can rapidly build up our content and user base. For music professionals and companies that want to replace their current web conferencing services e.g. WEBEX, with ours, we will be charging a subscription fee. Otherwise, our focus will be on the longer term revenue prospects of video content download sales and site advertising. Our current P & L forecast shows revenue in excess of $140 million in year 5 with EBITDA in the 60% range.

Industry Profile

- The age of the mega star is passing. Millions of bands are now competing for market share as the music industry continues to reinvent itself in the digital age.

- Digital communities and social networking sites are fundamentally changing the music business and the fan and artist relationship. There are currently 4,700,000 bands listed on Myspace.com with 130 million registered users.

- According to AccuStream, video streams viewed rose by 50.5% in 2005 to ~18 billion and are forecasted to grow by 32% in

2006 and 26% in 2007. Music videos accounted for 46% of the views. According to Neilsen in March of '06, the number of active broadband users in the U.S. has increased by 28% in the last year to 95.5 million.

- According to Streaming West Media, 500 million Internet streaming devices exist today and within 4 years, the number will grow to 1 billion. 94 million people are streaming videos of more than an hour long to their devices & one third of all Internet traffic is video.

- Digital music and video download sites are pervasive and growing rapidly. Portable music and video player options now include i-Pods and Cell phones. i-Tunes recently sold 8 million videos in just 3 months. YouTube streams 125 million videos per day to a user base of 72 million after just one year after their launch.

- Fans continually look for ways to meet their favorite artists and associate with them. It is a basic human emotion shared by millions of people.

YBR Summary Strategy

- Offer **BandDigs** to bands and fans for free to quickly build up content and users.

- Using the BandDigs platform/base investment, create and launch **FanDigs** (a site designed to support all types of celebrities)

- Develop additional strategic alliances with technology companies to further enhance the artist and fan relationship and music experience (bolt-ons to **BandDigs**).

- Fully monetize the **BandDigs** site and sell video & audio downloads of the chats/live broadcasts on our site. Distribute content to other sites e.g. i-Tunes

- Sell premium higher priced subscriptions to corporate clients.
- Sell low key advertising (Band video events branded, "Chatcasts" downloads/ watermarks), banner ads on chat/broadcast pages and on the website general pages.
- Offer revenue sharing to the bands.
- Broadcast live online video festivals/in store events (wrapped with sponsorships).
- Build an archived catalog of video recordings of events on **BandDigs**.

Financial Projections (excluding acquisitions)

- Year 1 = 5,250 subscribers, 1.5 million users, sales = $687K & EBITDA ($1.8 million)
- Year 3 = 21,000 subscribers, 7.3 million users, sales = $62 million & EBITDA $38 million
- Year 5 = 54,000 subscribers, 16.5 million users, sales = $145 million & EBITDA $90 million

Funding Approach

$4,000,000 is required to produce the following results in the next 12-18 months:

- Launch **BandDigs** broadly through viral marketing and other means
- Develop additional strategic alliances/partnerships
- Plan and build out the infrastructure to support user projections
- Establish the legal and accounting structure & recruit Advisory Board/BOD
- Hire additional staff (IT, Sales, Finance and Customer Service)

- Sell site subscriptions & sponsorships/advertising consistent with the financial plan
- Complete/file additional patents and trademark applications
- Build out the 2.0 broader celebrity release (**FanDigs**) including mobile initiative

Investor Requirements

Capital Investment:	**$4,000,000 Total**
Form:	YBR's Common/Preferred Stock

Use of Proceeds	
18 months of current burn rate	$ 750,000
IT Staff hired (12-18 months)	$ 500,000
Additional features 2.0 Release (FanDigs)	$ 200,000
Infrastructure planning & investments	$ 700,000
Sales and Marketing staff & promotion	$ 300,000
Legal, Finance, Admin & Office related	$ 300,000
Cell phone compatibility/pocket streaming	$ 150,000
Tools Licenses & Finance Application	$ 100,000
Working capital - general purpose	$ 1,000,000
Total Investment Requirement	**$ 4,000,000**

Exit Strategy

- Sell to larger music promotion/social networking entity like MSN, Yahoo, Google, Newscorp/Myspace, AOL, Ebay/Skype, Radio Disney, Clear Channel, Sony, etc.

Disclaimers

- This document is for information purposes only.
- This does not constitute an offer to sell or a solicitation of an offer to buy any securities to any person.
- In addition, this document may contain forward-looking statements. These statements are only predictions, are speculative and are not any guarantee of future results or performance.
- No warranty or guarantee is given regarding the accuracy, reliability, veracity, or completeness of the information provided here.

EXHIBIT I – NEW YORK ANGELS PRESENTATION

Yellow Brick Road Entertainment

Garry Wheeler - Founder & CEO/CTO
Revolutionizing the online relationship between celebrities & their fans

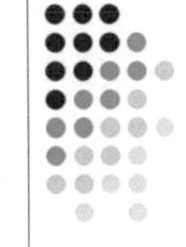

Vision

- To build a $350 million Web 2.0 product and services company over the next 5 years in the media, sports and entertainment industry

Our focus is on internet & mobile based "do it yourself" <u>live</u> & <u>interactive</u> <u>video</u> tools and communities for celebrity promotion.

In a Nutshell... Our platform:

- Supports 50 live webcams on one screen with a celebrity (online meet & greet)
- Allows a celebrity to run their own live and interactive global internet TV station in just 10 minutes (ad supported)
- Collects lots of very specific demographic data about fans
- Is a complement to My Space and You Tube (a logical extension), not a replacement

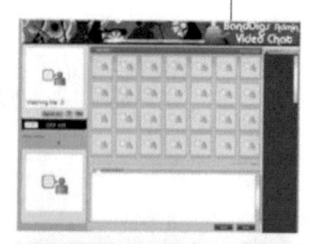

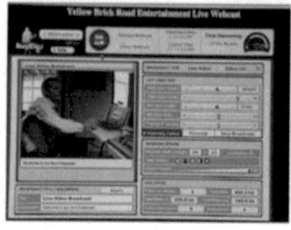

Meet Yellow Brick Road

Mgmt Team
- **Garry Wheeler – Founder/CEO** – is a 25+ year high tech industry veteran/Chief Information Officer and award winning entrepreneur with 7 years experience in the entertainment industry.
- **Richard Ellis – Strategic Marketing Consultant & Strategic Advisor** - has over 20 years in the entertainment industry (executive positions at Warner Music Group, Sony Music, BMG, Time Inc, Musician Magazine & Contemporary Productions).
- **Tracy Vail – Business Dev Manager** – former Clear Channel local artist marketing director, Manager of the band Angry Hill, former assistant to Al Kooper (Blood Sweat and Tears) and a Berklee Graduate.
- **Andria Goodrow – Artist Relations** – former touring support professional for Camplified tour, the Warped Tour, Take Action Tour, etc. with an emphasis on charity and artist relations.

Market Sizing (Drivers)

- ~200+ million people have accounts on (MySpace, YouTube, Facebook, etc.)
- 5.5 million band pages on MySpace alone & thousands of other celebrities are online
- Over $1 billion in online advertising forecasted for 2008 and growing rapidly
- Teens spend over $6 billion annually on entertainment

Pain Points ➡ Our Response

- Millions now competing for fan interest and loyalty where hundreds competed before
- Touring is very expensive

- The industry is looking for additional sources of revenue and new content
- CDs are not selling & labels are losing money
- Advertisers & fans are looking for the next big thing
- Keeping your information current on many sites is time consuming
- Users resist downloading special software

- Create a new bond with your fans by taking them backstage & allowing them to interact with you real time
- Perform globally from your own space for free
- Sell tickets to online events, share in ad $ from sponsors & sell copies of fan chats/videos
- Sell autographed merch/CDs during live events for higher prices
- Our platform revolutionizes the online relationship
- We integrate with You Tube & MySpace and support RSS feeds
- We are URL driven and work for PC and MAC

Top Level Business Strategies

- Market a few top artist big events
- Bands and fans are free, but offered fee based premium services
- Monetize the site through content sales and advertising
- Launch broader celebrity site (FanDigs) on same platform
- License the platform (white label) including ad services
- Acquire complementary businesses

~Sources of Revenue

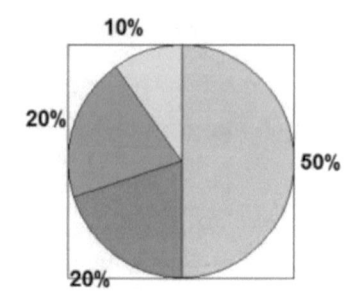

- Ads: 50%
- Content: 20%
- Services: 20%
- Subscrip: 10%

68% = through organic growth and 32% = through acquisitions

Customers *(in the millions)*

- Fans of any/all celebrities
- Musicians, recording artists, songwriters, producers & bands (signed and independent)
- Music related businesses (labels, managers, studios, venues, etc.)
- Pro athletes (all sports/levels)
- Sports management
- Actors
- Gamers
- Film producers
- Comedians
- Authors
- TV personalities
- Chefs
- Clothing designers
- Auto racing
- Politicians
- Religious leaders
- Advertisers of all types

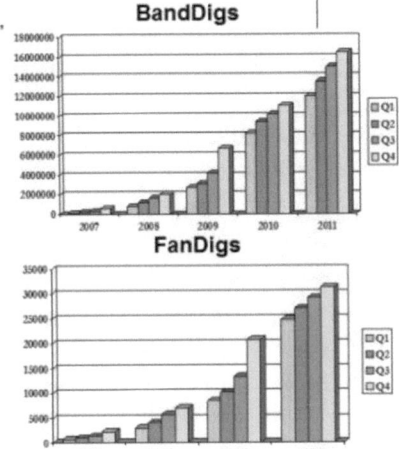

BandDigs

FanDigs

June 2007 G.S. Wheeler   YBR Entertainment Confidential   9

Current Alliances

EPIC · myxer tones · CROSSDOGS · nimbit · Daddy's Funky Music

MUSICGORILLA · fix8 · wiredset · 12 to 20 · FanBridge Email List Management for Bands

JAMSPOT [Let it out] · GEFFEN · Superdups.com CD & DVD DUPLICATION · Walt Disney Records

Virgin

June 2007 G.S. Wheeler   YBR Entertainment Confidential   10

Primary Competitors

- Stickam*
- Paltalk*
- Rehearsals.com
- Pure Volume**
- Hello World*
- AT & T Blue Room
- Grouper
- My Space**
- You Tube**

* More like us than the others
** Try to complement them vs. compete with them

Barriers to Entry

- Time to market - 12+ months of development effort
- Expense of retrofitting an existing site/architecture
- Artist & label relationships
- Patent Pending - Process & Method patent application

Financial Summary
(Assuming A Round & including acquisitions)

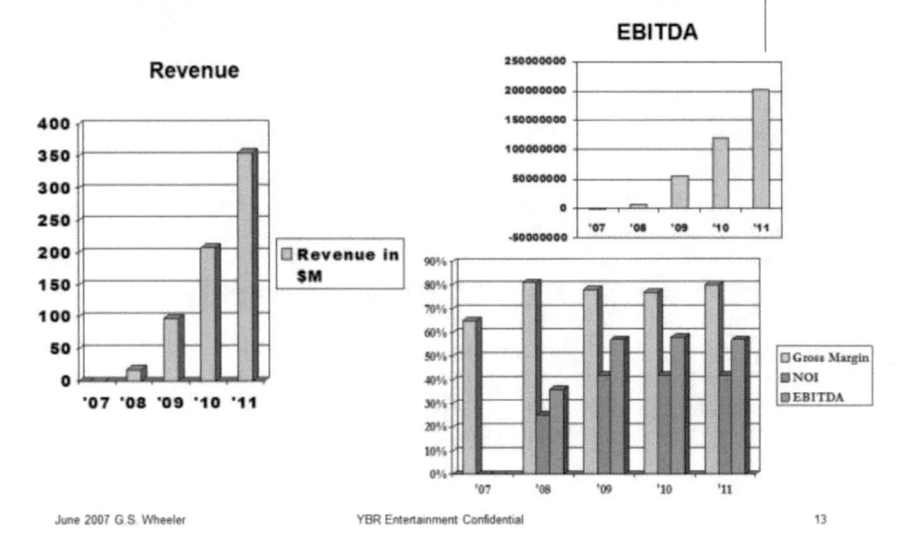

Revenue (Revenue in $M, '07–'11): values shown approximately 10, 95, 205, 350

EBITDA ('07–'11)

Gross Margin / NOI / EBITDA ('07–'11)

June 2007 G.S. Wheeler — YBR Entertainment Confidential

Bridge to A Round – Continue to commercialize while we go after $4-5 million

Use of A Round Funds		
6 months of current burn rate	$	200,000
IT Director hired (5 months)	$	45,000
White Label Development	$	30,000
Infrastructure planning & build out	$	50,000
Additional sales and marketing/promotion	$	100,000
Legal, Finance, Admin & Office related	$	25,000
Endorsement Deals with top artists	$	25,000
Software Licenses	$	25,000
Total Investment Requirement	$	500,000

June 2007 G.S. Wheeler — YBR Entertainment Confidential

Valuation - $500K bridge

- Pre-money = $3,000,000
- Post money = $3,500,000
- New Investor(s) ownership = ~14.3% (2.8% per $100,000)

- We raised $600,000 from six accredited individual investors one year ago and established a $2 million post valuation at that time.
- Founder owns 70% and each of the 6 individual investors owns 5% of the company.
- We have since built/launched the product, set up our infrastructure & team, registered ~400 professional musicians & 2000 fans (validating interest) & established many key strategic partnerships including several major labels and Daddy's Junky Music.

Summary

- Innovative Web 2.0 product that works now (platform based & built to scale)
- Very positive industry feedback & many new deals pending… we are not hearing "no"
- Solid base team in place (blend of technical and industry experience)
- Poised for very rapid growth

Platform Suite... BandDigs example

EXHIBIT J- 1244 STOCK LOSS PROVISION

http://cpa-services.com/special_qua.shtml
Qualified Small Business Stock & 1244 Stock – Riley Associates P.C. – Newburyport, Mass.

By Peter Jason Riley

Section 1244 of the Internal Revenue Code, the small business stock provision, was enacted to allow shareholders of domestic small business corporations to deduct as ordinary losses, losses sustained when they dispose of their small business stock. In order to receive this beneficial treatment, the Code prescribes specific requirements for: (1) the corporation issuing the small business stock; (2) the stock itself; and (3) the shareholders of the corporation.

(1) The corporation issuing the stock must qualify as a domestic small business corporation, which generally means that it must be created under the laws of the United States and that its aggregate capital must not exceed $1,000,000 at the time the §1244 stock is issued to its shareholders. The first taxable year in which the capital of the corporation exceeds $1,000,000 is called the transitional year, and the corporation must designate which shares issued that year qualify for §1244. For example, if a newly formed corporation received $2,000,000 for its initial issue of stock, it could designate up to $1,000,000 of its stock as qualified §1244 stock.

The corporation must also satisfy a gross receipts test. This test requires that the corporation, during the period of its five most recent years ending before the date the loss on its stock was sustained, derive more than 50% of its gross receipts from sources other than passive investment income. The gross receipts test thereby confines the tax relief provided by the small business stock provision to the stock of corporations actively engaged in a trade or business. The gross receipts test does not apply where, for the entire period for which gross receipts are measured, the gross income of the corporation is less than the business deductions allowed to the corporation by the Code.

The Code also imposes recordkeeping requirements on the corporation relative to its §1244 stock. Among these is requirement that the corporation designate designation, for its transitional year, those of its outstanding shares that qualify for small business stock treatment.

(2) Common stock, and preferred stock issued after July 18, 1984, qualifies as §1244 stock. In order to qualify as §1244 stock, the stock must be issued, and the consideration paid by the shareholder must consist of money or other property, not services. Stock and other securities are not "other property" for this purpose. However, cancellation of indebtedness may be sufficiently valid consideration.

(3) Section 1244 is available only for losses sustained by shareholders who are individuals. Losses sustained on stock held by a corporation, trust or estate do not qualify for §1244 treatment. Subject to very limited exceptions, the benefits of §1244 are only available to individuals who acquire the stock by issuance from a domestic small business corporation, and are not available to a subsequent transferee of the stock. In some cases, a partnership can qualify as a shareholder of §1244 stock. Generally, all transfers of §1244 stock by the shareholder, whether in a taxable or nontaxable transaction, whether by death, gift, sale or exchange, terminate §1244 status.

Once all of the requirements of §1244 stock are met, ordinary loss treatment for losses on a sale or exchange of §1244 stock is permitted if the loss would otherwise be treated as a capital loss. The amount of ordinary loss that an individual taxpayer may realize by reason of the small business stock provision is subject to certain limitations. Any amount of §1244 loss in excess of this limitation is treated as a capital loss. For losses incurred in taxable years beginning after 1978, the maximum amount that a taxpayer may claim as an ordinary loss for all losses sustained on §1244 stock in a taxable year is $50,000, generally, or $100,000 if a joint return is filed.

Because the rules under §1244 are complicated, I encourage you to contact your tax advisor how they apply to your situation.

LINKS TO VIDEOS THAT SHOW BANDDIGS.COM TOOLS AND PROMOTION

My Book Site

http://www.ybrentertainment.net

My BLOG

http://www.garrywheeler.com

Webcast Tool Demo

http://www.youtube.com/watch?v=1xrcMO4R2Zk

50+ Person Video Chat Demo

http://www.youtube.com/watch?v=ubn3Xa3KXcw

General Promo Video

http://www.youtube.com/watch?v=lFojgduFag4

Jada Promo Video

http://www.youtube.com/watch?v=hN4g_DyFgTA

Old Myspace Page

http://www.myspace.com/banddigs

EXAMPLE OF ONE OF OUR MANY PROMOTIONS

BandDigs

www.banddigs.com

NEW MUSIC ONLY WEBSITE LAUNCHES, GIVING BANDS GLOBAL EXPOSURE, FANS UNPRECEDENTED ACCESS

Bands & Musicians,

We would like to introduce you to a new and unique online community that is revolutionizing the way bands and fans communicate. BandDigs.com offers bands the technology to broadcast your shows, rehearsals, recording sessions, backstage events, interviews, etc. live over the Internet any time that you want. All you need is a computer, a high speed Internet connection and a video camera or webcam.

But, here's the really cool thing about BandDigs.com, we provide you with the tools to host group video chats where you can talk face to face with your fan base all from one website without any special software. Many independent artists like Violet Nine, Angry Hill, Fort Pastor and Jillian Wheeler are already on the site. As well as signed bands like Over It (Virgin), Black Rebel Motorcycle Club (RCA), Reggie and the Full Affect (Vagrant), Punchline (Fueled by Raman), Jada (Motown) and Aberdeen City (Columbia).

There is a lot more to the story.... We invite you to check out BandDigs.com and get involved now. **The site is free to bands and to their fans so please go and register today!**

BandDigs.com, Musician Tested, Fan Friendly!

MY PLEADING TO OUR SUBSCRIBER BASE

Hey Everyone,

I am the Founder of BandDigs.com and I am sending this note to ask you for your help.

We have close to 400 bands and businesses that have registered on BandDigs since we launched and barely any of you have tried to use the tools. In fact, many of you have not even built your page or published it so fans can find you.

We have called many of you and you tell us that you still plan on using the site.... Well if this is true, why not do something in the next couple of weeks? The only way that our site will take off so that we can afford to give everyone the free use of our live video broadcast tool, our video blog and our video chat space is if a lot of you start to use these tools. Our revenue model is primarily based on us selling advertising. We in turn plan to share ad revenue with all of you, but until we have a lot of events going on and a lot of fans signing up for the community, we can't charge for advertising.

Believe me when I tell you, our site costs a lot of money each month to keep running. We have lots of hardware, bandwidth, software licenses and people supporting the site whether you use it or not. We can't keep the site alive if we don't generate some revenue to offset these expenses.

So, I am asking you all to help us. Log into your account, click on Edit My Page and then go the webcast or vchat tab. Schedule the use of one of the tools. Just pick a time an hour later and try playing with one of the tools. Go back into your account when it is time to start your event and click on the start button on the same page that you scheduled the use of the tool with. You can't break the tools, so just play with them. The broadcast tool and v-chat tool shows up in your account only when you schedule the use of them. The Video Blog tool is always available in your account. You don't need to invite your fans, just play with the tools a little. See what is involved. Better yet, come to a free online training session and learn how to use the tools from us. All you need is a webcam to use any of the tools on our site. You can buy a webcam these days for $15 to $25.

Within 10 minutes you can be your own live Internet TV station… you can even broadcast pre-recorded videos and then talk to your fans about the video if you prefer. Whatever you do live using the tool you can record and make available later as a download and/or you can re-broadcast it as many times as you want. You can hook up your webcam, click on the V-Blog tab and click one button to record a video message that will show up on your page. With our chat space, you can have up to 20 fans online with you and you can control the discussion. The fan's audio only turns on when you accept a question from them. Our new chat space can handle 50 fans with even more watching and will allow you to record fan conversations.

We have had a few bands take their fans backstage live, on their tour bus and into the recording studio with them. This is what your fans want to see! These same bands have broadcasted some live shows, taken their fans into their rehearsal spaces and then answered questions from fans like an interactive TV show. You could even just turn the camera on and interview each other and let your fans watch.

My team is here to help you with the technology, but we need your help using it and inviting your fans to join or we won't be here for very long. Let us know if you have problems or concerns… you can give us feedback by sending e-mail to support@banddigs.com . We read and respond to every e-mail that we get.

We are planning some events of our own and a major marketing campaign that will run this summer. Your band will get the benefit of this promotion if your page is published and you schedule some type of event.

Start small, but please go for it… if nothing else, you'll learn something new!

Garry

Garry Wheeler
Founder & CEO
Yellow Brick Road Entertainment LLC
BandDigs.com
Musician Tested, Fan Friendly!

Hippo Press Article

Connecting bands to fans

Online community changes communication platform
By Erica Febre efebre@hippopress.com

Move over, Myspace, and say hello to BandDigs, a new online community dedicated to musicians and their fans. Yellow Brick Road Entertainment, based in Windham, is the creator of this one-of-a-kind interactive community.

"Our goal was to provide bands with interactive technology once only afforded by large corporations that would enable them to take their careers to the next level," said Garry Wheeler, founder and CEO of Yellow Brick.

Those already working the platform provided by Myspace are aware of the limited capabilities - add friends, view profiles, post bulletins and blogs. For the regular, non-music-related user, this may seem like more than enough. But for bands and their fans, the one thing that's missing is live interaction.

"We wanted to take the concept of an online social community to a new level. Literally, within minutes of subscribing to BandDigs, a band can be broadcasting live around the world like they own a TV station, or they can be interacting with their audience face to face," Wheeler said.

The site offers video streaming, online interactive chatting, and a very large database that allows bands and fans to upload, store and save music videos. Fans can talk to their favorite bands face to face using a webcam. They can also provide feedback about shows, songs, videos or albums. They even get points for promoting their favorite bands and drawing in new fans. The best part is that bands can make live performances available for fans everywhere.

For instance, Angry Hill might have a show in New York that fans in New Hampshire wish they could catch. Angry Hill could make that show a live broadcast from BandDigs and fans could watch it from their own homes.

"The best thing is, you can see us from anywhere and at anytime. I think this is gonna be killer and the fans are gonna love it," said Keith Denehy of Angry Hill.

Why hasn't this been done before? There are a few big corporations using online communities like this to conduct business. But as far as the music industry is concerned, it's been just too expensive to consider, especially for the musicians, let alone the fans.

"A band would be hard-pressed to try and figure out how to even make the technology for themselves. It takes a lot of development, plus you have to buy a lot of licenses to plug into that and then you've got to serve it up in a very big, robust way on the Internet," Wheeler said.

"It's a combination of those things [that] makes it very unaffordable, even to an individual record label. We have lots of very, very powerful servers to get this working," Wheeler said.

BandDigs already has some major artists signed up from record labels such as Virgin Records, RCA, Motown, Columbia and more. A number of local New England bands are also taking advantage of BandDigs.

At the moment, the service is free to bands as well as fans. Signing up costs nothing, but doesn't include charges that may be incurred by bands posting a live broadcast. Bands may make shows available to fans for free or they may charge.

Fans will also be able to record their favorite broadcasts in a database stored on the site (so it won't bog down home computers). The only application that may be required is the latest version of Flash Media. Other than that, the site provides all utilities needed to make things run smoothly.

This is only the beginning of the online community that literally will revolutionize the way bands communicate with their fans. Changes and additions are in the works as more fans and bands join.

Yellow Brick will also present BandDigs at a February program at New Hampshire's High-Technology Council's MIT Enterprise Forum. The session will take place on Thursday, Feb. 8, starting at 5:30 p.m. at First Place located in the Manchester Millyard.

Online

Who: BandDigs.com

What: online community for bands and their fans

When: MIT Enterprise Forum on Thursday, Feb. 8, starting at 5:30 p.m.

Where: First Place in the Manchester Millyard

For more information: Go to BandDigs.com to register as a band or a fan. For more information on the forum, go to www.nhhtc.org

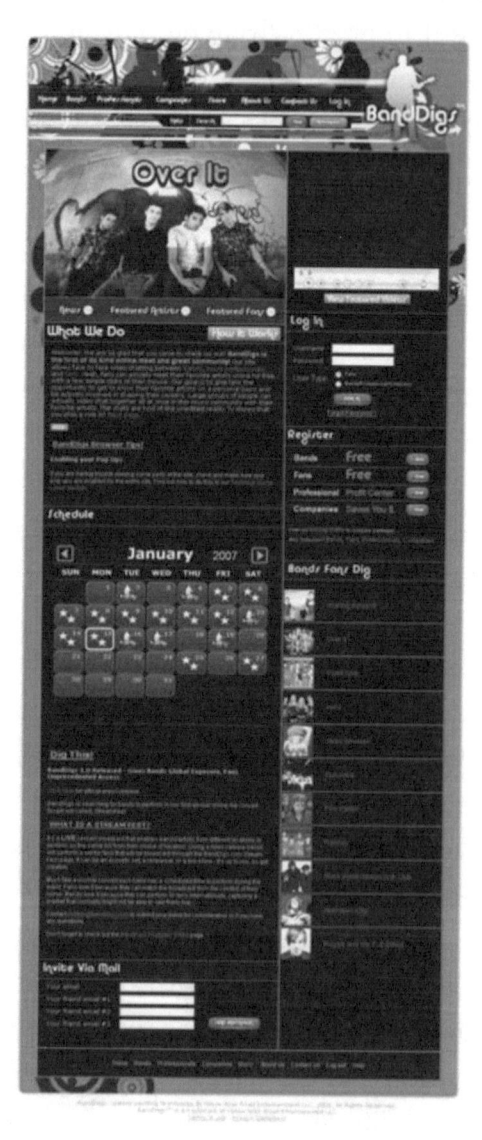

Made in the USA
Columbia, SC
15 July 2024